POWER TO EXCEL

POWER TO EXCEL

With A "How To" Formula
$$C(P + Q + D) = AQ \ ©$$

Hubert E. Dobson

Rich Publishing Co.
Houston, Texas 77070

ISBN 0-9607256-1-X
Library of Congress Catalog Card No. 81-90553
Published by: Rich Publishing Company
                    Houston, Texas

Printed in the United States of America

Acknowledgments

I want to thank all those who have encouraged me to put my experiences, philosophies and beliefs in writing for the benefit of others.

Acknowledgment is hereby made to the publishers and authors of books, articles and poems for permission to quote passages or excerpts. Any errors that may have inadvertently occurred will be corrected in future editions, on request.

I am indebted to many devotees for their generous help in preparing the manuscript: Jeanne Haines and Elizabeth Dobson for typing and advising; my children Sherry, Barry, Mary, Debbie for their encouragement. Finally, my gratitude goes to my dear wife Helen, to whom this book is dedicated.

HUBERT E. DOBSON

Introduction

The Purpose

The future belongs to things that grow whether it be in nature or man. Human growth and progress is a result of change. This book is written for all who want to grow in life, to be a high achiever in the quest to serve self and mankind. It is intended to serve the reader as a helpful guide to reach desired levels of achievement. A guide is a tool for use and reference today and tomorrow. Let it become just that. Read, reread, mark the pages to serve you as a reference for progress. The aspirations and desires of all who are dissatisfied with their level of achievement can be fulfilled with diligent application of the principles outlined. Your desire may be to obtain a greater share of life's riches and personal happiness. It may be money, love, admiration, mental, physical, social, spiritual growth. These riches can be yours—and more. It does not depend on your education, your current status or even luck. You have within you the potential power to achieve the things you really want. You can grow. You can reach out and excel.

A Formula for Achievement

I will unfold the ingredients of a power laden formula that can lead you to higher levels of achievement. The formula is a result of many years experience in management, sales, production, communications and related roles in business and industry. Each role involved a close association with many people as indeed most roles do. Growth and progress in my experience stems not so much from what one does for himself, although that is important, as it does from what the person does for others. Application of the power formula will serve as a stimulus, a model of the basic elements one needs to become a satisfied achiever. As you apply the formula you will be challenged to reach for greatness in your chosen field of interest or activity.

An Unseen Force

Life's ladder of achievement and happiness is held in balance by a delicate unseen force. The ladder will stand at the exact angle for easy climbing when you harmonize your talents, abilities and interests with the needs and interests of others. If you are unable to climb your ladder then the angle for climbing is askew. Something is out of balance. Something in your life is out of harmony with the needs and interests of others. It is said that ninety-five percent of our problems stem from within. We are the cause. Thus if problems do exist, there is a good chance you will find solutions by first looking within yourself. After carefully and thoroughly searching within, then and only then consider looking at the external forces.

The Plan

The book sets forth a plan to help you develop and use your innate power to achieve, to be successful. Whatever your ambition, goal, or desire, the end result will in some way influence the lives of others. Strangely, people are usually more interested in themselves and in their success than anything else. Yet, personal success is dependent on others. Success in a field of endeavor is the desire of most people. Some achieve it easily. Some have it handed to them on a platter. Some succeed only after much effort, patience, and determination. Some never do.

Success Is!

What is success? It has been defined in many ways. Earl Nightingale writes: Success is "The progressive realization of a worthy ideal." "Optimizing one's God given talents" is another suggestion. There are recorded successes, depending on your choice of definition in every field. It may be a housewife and mother performing her daily tasks with skill, feeling, and happiness. It may be a teacher, helping children grow and develop. It may be a sports figure thrilling audiences with a display of great skill. People invariably excel in the roles they enjoy most. "What you're doing ain't work unless you would rather be doing something else," said Will Rogers. Success in every activity or role being played in life is dependent on an end user of the output. As the humorist Josh Billings used to say, "Them iz people."

Efforts Must Benefit Others

Visualize that every action, game, service or product you generate will be for people. The road to accomplishment takes on a different prospective when you stop to realize that all your efforts are really for the benefit of others. Your payoff is in the acceptance by others of what you do. You may work in entertainment. You may farm or work in a factory. Your office may be on a side street or in a modern skyscraper. The type of product or service performed would make an endless list. The end user is always the same—

and "them iz people." The primary difference in one's success or failure in a chosen venture is frequently in the personal relationships with people. There is a presence or absence of feeling or COMPASSION for those being served. I watched the launching of a new restaurant that had all the outward appearance of a successful venture. There was standing room only for all meals during the first week. In three months, the doors closed due to lack of customers. People were saying the facility was first class; food was choice and the prices right. But the owner and staff were so unpleasant to deal with that customers did not return. The business changed hands. The new owners are now operating a successful business. They realize the end user of their service is people.

A Course of Action

The course you choose to pursue will involve some type of PREPARATION. That is, education for knowledge; training to develop skills; personal development for general awareness. Business and industry recruiters seek personnel with academic degrees to fill most salaried administrative and technical positions. Experience is a key factor in most office clerical and blue collar jobs. The degree of preparation therefore becomes the barometer for evaluation and selection. Advance planning for any role including marriage, rearing a family, buying a home or pursuing retirement has a better chance of success with adequate preparation.

Demand for your product or service will be in direct proportion to its QUALITY. People search for the best affordable quality in all goods and services. Employers prefer to hire personnel that possess quality characteristics. Top quality performers receive promotions, become tomorrow's leaders, earn top dollars. Products and services labelled top quality by consumers lead the field. Television, theater, sports, are top attractions when quality is present. Top quality performers are top achievers. Why? They render a service that satisfies the end user—people.

The manner or method by which you give, offer, sell, and DELIVER the product or service rendered will be judged by the people served. They will either like, dislike, or perhaps tolerate, the service, depending on the competitive services available. If people like your service and method of delivery, then further association and business could be expected. If people dislike the way they are served, they will probably search for alternatives. The absence of a better service may force people to tolerate poor service, but time will invariably allow other choices.

The Formula

Four key words that comprise your achievement level have been revealed. The following formula reflects their application for fulfillment:

$$C\,(P + Q + D) = AQ \, ©$$

The formula says COMPASSION for people multiplied by the sum total of PREPARATION + QUALITY + DELIVERY system equals ACHIEVEMENT QUOTIENT. Study the formula carefully. Memorize it. Reflect on the words deeply. Diligent and thoughtful application will provide an atomic capsule of energy to propel you to reach out for greatness and to achieve your impossible dream.

It is apparent that no word in the formula stands alone. Whether the product or service is offered by a single person or a corporate giant, the user will sense the degree of concern or COMPASSION for people. PREPARATION is of limited value unless it is supported by QUALITY. The best product or service will have limited demand unless the method of DELIVERY satisfies users. The combination of these ingredients will inevitably reflect your ACHIEVEMENT QUOTIENT in life.

Life's Riches and Happiness

You can be as great or as successful as you choose to be. Often, daily routines force people into a conforming mold of "what is" because it satisfies the basic necessities. Complacency and procrastination soon take over and the desire to excel is lost. The mental force that causes people to reach for greatness begins to weaken. What could be now seems unreachable. Indecisions, mental stagnation displace action. People cease to become. They are content just to be.

If your choice is to reach out for more of life's riches and personal happiness, to become and just not to be, then this book is for you. Read on. Build a higher ACHIEVEMENT QUOTIENT in your mental, physical, social, and spiritual gymnasium. Become the person you are really capable of being.

Question Review

Throughout this book chapter sections begin with a pertinent question. These serve as thought stimulators as you read and digest the contents.

All questions are again listed in the appendix, in chapter sequence, for review and possible further study. Upon completion of the book reexamine the questions and assess the need to reread a particular chapter, a section or the entire book.

Power to Excel
Contents

			Page
Acknowledgments			v
Introduction			vii

Chapter

1 **Humanity Power** (COMPASSION) **1**

● Reap a Bountiful Harvest ● Change Attitude to Gain Altitude ● Overcome Self-Concern ● Understand Yourself ● Discover What People Want ● Develop a Caring Attitude ● Be a Worthy Model ● Motivate Others to Excel ● Walk in the Other Fellow's Moccasins ● Help People Help Themselves

2 **Mind Power** (PREPARATION) **23**

● Discover Your Power Reservoir ● Develop Your Talents and Abilities ● Think Believe and Achieve ● Build a Character Image of Success ● Tune in Your Subconscious

3 **Want Power** (PREPARATION) **37**

Analyze Your Problems ● Set Definite Goals ● Develop Action Plans ● Share Your Goals and Plans ● Plant Seeds of Expectancy

4   Imagery Power   (PREPARATION)   51

● See Yourself Becoming ● Control Input and Output ● Bury Negative Thoughts ● Take off the Blinders ● Dress for Where You Are Going

5   Fitness Power   (PREPARATION)   65

● Go for Total Physical Fitness ● Apply Common Sense Principles ● Enjoy the Company of Others ● Count Your Blessings ● Balance Your Style

6   Resource Power   (PREPARATION)   81

● Build a Resource Gymnasium ● Get Your Act Together ● Use Your Creative Imagination ● Develop a Cooperative Spirit ● Adopt Attitude of Tolerance

7   Communication Power   (PREPARATION)   97

● Speak Your Way to Success ● Know What Audiences Expect ● Build Presentations in Logical Steps ● Master Effective Characteristics ● Use Humor Wisely ● Magnify with Visual Aids ● Evaluate Your Progress ● Get Results in Group Meetings

8   Competence Power   (QUALITY)   117

● Build on Your Qualifications ● Assume Responsibility for Actions ● Work Smarter Not Harder ● Build a Results Oriented Reputation ● Give Generous Measures ● Adapt to Changes ● Go an Extra Mile ● Keep Your Eyes on Finances ● Develop Subordinates ● Practice the Golden Rule

9   Personality Power   (DELIVERY)   143

● Magnify Your Potential ● Radiate Your Personality ● Become a Good Conversationalist ● Make Lasting Impressions ● Avoid Making Enemies

10   Enthusiasm Power   (DELIVERY)   161

● Get Excited About Life ● Illuminate with Action ● Spread Optimism ● Reinforce Your Incentives ● Kindle a Fire of Joy

CONTENTS

11   **Self-Esteem Power**   (DELIVERY)   **175**

● Be Introspective ● Evaluate Your Self-Esteem ● Increase Your Awareness ● Feel Good About Yourself ● Take Charge of Your Life

12   **Self-Confidence Power**   (DELIVERY)   **189**

● Believe in Yourself ● Walk Tall ● Set Higher Standards ● Make Accurate Decisions ● Build Confidence in Others

13   **Persistence Power**   (DELIVERY)   **207**

● Keep Your Battery Charged ● Respond to Weaknesses ● Concentrate on Best Results ● Be Patient ● Never Despair

14   **Success Power**   (ACHIEVEMENT QUOTIENT)   **223**

● Adopt Reasons for Achievement ● Commit Yourself to Do Great Things ● Fulfill Your Aspirations ● Pursue Worthwhile Ventures ● Set 5 Year Growth Plans ● Launch Your Ship ● Make Happiness Your Pilot ● Keep Your Eyes on the Little Things ● Build a Success Consciousness ● Use Power Wisely

APPENDIX   **253**
QUESTION REVIEW   **253**

1
Humanity Power

Man may dismiss compassion from his heart, but God never will.
—Wm. Cowper

(COMPASSION)

Do you have COMPASSION for people?
It is a reflection of your deepest feelings: kindness, consideration, gentleness, indulgence, tenderness, and readiness to help people.
Do you demonstrate COMPASSION for people?
This implies that you pursue daily actions or expressions of honest feelings, favors, benevolence, tolerance, generosity, and unselfishness toward people. If so, you either are or can be a high achiever. Conversely, if you do not have COMPASSION for people or the ability to show it, your achievement level will be adversely affected.

The world of every human being revolves around people, feelings for them, the treatment given and, in turn, their response. Your world is a continual association with people. The manner in which you pursue these-day-to-day associations represents the building blocks of personal achievement and happiness.

You started life as a unique human being. You represent

1

the highest form of creation in the universe. Within you is the physical, mental, social, and spiritual makeup that shapes your destiny. You possess unlimited ability to reach out and shape the world of your desires. The seeds of an inborn power are in every animal and await recognition. When this unlimited power potential becomes evident, you need only apply and channel it correctly to raise your achievement level beyond imagination.

Begin today to realize that the power of humanity is unlimited. Whatever awesome power may be envisioned, it will invariably be triggered by or through human minds. Therefore, is it not within the realm of existence to make better use of this power—to increase your achievement level?

Recognize from this point forward that whatever good fortune has or may come your way, it will doubtless have been influenced by others. It may have been parents, relatives, marriage partner, friends, co-workers, minister, priest, or rabbi. People will have had something to do with the accomplishments. As the amount of human influence increases, the level of achievement will increase. This influence may be in the form of help or guidance to produce a product or service. It may be counseling or just a word of encouragement. In any event, people will be involved. COMPASSION toward those people, whether they help to produce or consume the end product, will influence your AQ (Achievement Quotient).

Reap a Bountiful Harvest

Are you satisfied with your achievement level today?

If so, it is the result of the seeds planted yesterday. If not, the answer is probably the same—the seeds planted yesterday. Tomorrow's harvest will be the result, good or ill, of the seeds sown today. "From the same materials one builds palaces and another hovels; one rears a stately edifice, while his brother, vacillating and incompetent, lives forever amid ruins," advocated Henry Ward Beecher.

Yes! It makes a difference where and how the seeds of life are planted. My early experience in planting seeds occurred during boyhood on an Illinois grain farm. The land was rich fertile black loam that, with care, would produce abundant crops of corn, soybeans, and wheat. A shallow creek crossed one section of the farm. Water flowed in its bed during heavy rains. While we seeded the dry creek bed at planting time, the rains always seemed to beat us to the harvest. Ultimately, the creek bed was sown in grass to prevent land erosion. We learned to plant seeds only where the opportunity for greatest growth existed. If you expect to reap bountiful benefits of personal efforts, plant seeds where the opportunity for greatest growth exists.

Before modern agriculture machinery existed, it was common practice to broadcast seeds by hand or with simple rotary seeders. While grain production was good in that era, there is no comparison with today's high productivity as a result of controlled planting. Grains are now planted in precise quantities under controlled conditions with sophisticated machinery.

Broadcasting one's efforts in many fields with outdated methods will not produce the best results. While life responds generously to generous doers, the opportunities are usually greatest in a single field of endeavor. Specialized knowledge can be cultivated and applied. Skills can be practiced and developed.

Henry Ford, the pioneer of automobile manufacturers, achieved great success in producing the Model T Ford. On one occasion when interviewed by the media he was asked, "To what do you attribute your success in automobile production?" He replied, "I stuck with the same model." The seeds he planted were carefully cultivated and controlled.

Remember that the seeds you plant in life will be influenced by or utilized by people. Life is people and you are one of the fold. Plant selectively, cultivate carefully. Harvest

3

with deep concern for people; those that help you along the way and those that will benefit from your efforts.

Compassion for people adds meaning to your life.

Change Attitude to Gain Altitude

Do you have a positive attitude toward achievement?

The heights to which you envision climbing will be measured by the depth of your feelings and thinking about life itself. This represents attitude and, in turn, controls altitude of achievement. Physical endowments are inherited from ancestors, but you alone are responsible for your attitude toward others. In turn, others' attitudes toward you are dependent on your attitude toward them.

The achievement formula on which this book is written is framed around attitude toward all things. It will be apparent that the right mental approach to people is all important to achievement. Likewise, the attitude toward preparation, quality, and delivery of any product or service will influence the end results. In turn, one's achievement quotient will rise or fall as attitude changes occur. Thus, you can change your AQ by changing your attitude of mind.

William James declared that "the greatest revolution in his generation was the discovery that human beings, by changing the inner attitudes of their minds, can change the outer aspects of their lives."

The primary ingredient in a pleasant, productive attitude toward all things is harmony. That is, harmonizing your frame of mind with the work you do and the people with whom you associate.

Compare the need for harmony in a choir, quartet or other singing group. Or consider the need to blend instruments in an orchestra, combo or any musical group. Anyone that sings or plays off-key is creating disturbing sounds, arousing the emotions of associates and the audience. The offender will need to shape up, get in tune, or drop out.

Consider the value of harmony in a management team, a political party, a department of employees, a sports team or a family. Any member can inflict unbelievable havoc through a negative, dissident attitude. It takes only one member of the team to create discord and resultant disharmony.

A productive attitude is a harmonious one. Attitude is based in the seat of one's thought process. Thoughts are the only things over which you really have control. Thus, you can produce harmony or discord with either positive or negative thinking.

A positive attitude generates a wholesome spirit that is enjoyed by everyone; the negative attitude immediately colors the environment, and rains destruction on all relationships.

One of the toughest things to do is to think positive. It is so easy to jump the track and think negatively. The air waves are full of influence including news, people problems and the myriad of troubles that provoke society. The clue for living, feeling, thinking and acting positive is to eliminate negative thoughts. This can be done by (1) always substituting a positive thought when you hear a negative one (2) closing the door of your mind on negative thoughts—don't let them in.

The greatest challenge and opportunity today is in adopting an attitude of mind that builds harmony in all phases of your activities. Search for solutions to any hang-ups that seem to interfere with accomplishment. Spend your valued time on the issues which you can control. Attitude is one thing you can definitely control—a positive take off will allow you to continually gain altitude.

Compassion for people is a gauge of attitude.

Overcome Self-Concern

Is your greatest concern for others?
Most people have partial ownership in radio station WIIFM, "What's In It For Me." These interests were acquired

5

at birth. Children are basically selfish. They demonstrate self-ish concern for toys, playthings, the high chair, and anything called "mine." They worry about others playing with their possessions or infringing upon their territory. Animal instinct is evident. Dogs, large and small, quickly establish territorial claims along imaginary perimeters of a yard. If you have deep self-concern, attribute it to infantile behavior and a bit of animal instinct that can and must be overcome to achieve productive people relationships.

Self-concern is a common human characteristic. Worry, anxiety, stress, and tension are reflections of inner feelings. These can be destructive, but not all self-concern is bad. Personal goals, dress, values, and pride in the things you represent are valid concerns. Then, "How can I achieve a happy balance in life" you ask? To the extent that you convert your self-concern into concern for others you will be able to gain essential cooperation from people and raise your AQ (Achievement Quotient).

While serving as an army officer, training gun crews for service aboard cargo vessels, I had a lesson in self-concern. I was very worried about a young soldier in one crew. He did not seem to realize his responsibility, so I made a special effort to impress him. I told him that if he failed in his job the ship and its expensive cargo might be lost. Not only that, some of the men were highly trained; it cost Uncle Sam many dollars to train each of them. They might be killed through neglect. "So it is very important that you do your job properly; the gun crews must function as a team. Your neglect could cause the loss of this expensive ship, the cargo, and all these men," I said. "Yes sir, and then there's me, too," replied the soldier. My self-concern faded and I stopped worrying.

First Lady, Eleanor Roosevelt, speaking about self-con-cern, said "Like most older people, I am constantly fighting the temptation to slip into self-absorption. If one loses inter-est in the people who tie one to life, then it is very easy to lose interest in the world as a whole. Perhaps the most

6

important thing is to keep alive our love for others and to believe that our love and interest are as vitally necessary to them as to us."

Compassion for people softens the voice of self-concern.

Understand Yourself

Do you make a serious effort to understand yourself?

If so, I compliment you. Obviously you have planned your journeys with good logic and know the routes that lead to achievement. You will have made the great discovery that people avoid the emotionally influenced type, but are eager and waiting to help or follow the one who uses good judgment. If not, then there are hurdles to be overcome. Few people will have the confidence to join the illogical thinker on an uncertain journey.

There is no substitute for an accurate assessment of yourself to maximize your potential, particularly people relationships. Goethe, noted German poet and philosopher suggested: "The person with insight enough to admit his limitations comes nearest to perfection."

The manner in which you influence those around you has a significant effect on your achievement level. People are always reacting to each other either positively, negatively or passively. Thus, understanding the way you come through to others is important.

You are forever confronted with two major forces of influence—emotion and logic. Emotional response is seen as reaction; logical response is considered sensible action. Fortunately you have complete control over these forces. The choice to act or react is always yours.

Spontaneous reaction might be described as childlike. It typifies the child that always wants his way regardless of the discomfort heaped upon others. Sensible action reflects the judgment of a mature person that responds with sound logic, a well-thought-out plan that shows concern for the effect on others.

Babies express feelings or emotions by crying, screaming, or kicking to fulfill their desires. Depending on parental influence the learning curve of improved behavior can be gradual or steep. I was reared by parents who believed in strict discipline and hard work—both at an early age. I quickly discovered the benefits of good behavior. The payoff for using good judgment was always more pleasant than the penalty for emotional tactics.

Childhood influences are carried into adulthood. It is not unusual to witness or be involved in adult scenes that are reminiscent of childlike behavior. For instance political factions are noted for emotional childlike responses to suggestions of the opposition. Employees react to employer organization changes or new polices with negativism rather than logic.

You probably experience daily examples of emotional reaction vs logical action in the family, at work or in social environment. Pause and assess these two situations: Action based on logic; reaction based on emotion. Which would you rather deal with? Which produces the most beneficial results? You will no doubt quickly discover that the most mileage will be gained in using good logic.

Now apply this same assessment to your daily activities to determine those actions that are most productive for you. "The proof of the pudding is in the eating." I believe that sensible action rather than emotional reaction to any situation will definitely raise your achievement level.

Compassion for people stimulates continual assessment of personal motives.

Discover What People Want

Do you know what you want out of life?
Answer that question and you will probably discover there is a profound similarity in wants among all people.

The late Dr. Abraham Maslow, distinguished psychologist, suggested the entire human species has common and apparently unchanging psychological needs. These needs form a hierarchy, urgency or importance starting with the physical needs for air, water, food, shelter, sleep, and sex. Basic needs of safety and security follow. Then the hierarchy ranks love and belongingness followed by self-esteem and esteem by others, then growth needs, thereafter self-actualization.

Frank Goble, former associate of Dr. Maslow and author of *Excellence in Leadership* (copyright 1972 by the Thomas Jefferson Research Center and published by Caroline House), writes, "Dr. Maslow made a distinction between the basic needs, which he called 'deficiency needs' and the 'growth needs' or 'higher needs.' He believed that the higher nature of man required the lower nature as a foundation and, without this foundation, the higher nature collapsed. The major emphasis in humanistic psychology, he stated, rests on the assumptions regarding 'higher needs.' They are seen as biologically based, part of the human essence. People who achieve a higher degree of self-actualization behave in a different way than the majority. Rather than struggling with life, these actualized people are more spontaneous, expressive, natural, and free, almost as if they have gotten to the top of the hill and are now coasting down the other side. The higher needs are not in a hierarchy. All are of equal value and are interrelated. Maslow estimated that only a tiny percentage, certainly less than 2% of the human race, ever achieved self-actualization." Self-actualized people, Maslow found, have the following characteristics:

Purposeful	Considerate	Self-disciplined
Realistic	Ethical	Self-confident
Creative	Spontaneous	Integrated
Humble	Courageous	

"Industrial research seems to indicate that achievement is a basic need," according to Frank Goble. "People have a need to achieve, which is slightly different from Maslow's need to grow or self-actualize. Maslow himself found that people need purpose. All his self-actualized people had it. Isn't it logical to assume that purpose is a basic need?"

The basic thread woven among the words of learned theorists is that people have a need to achieve. People accept roles of great responsibility, work endless hours, accomplish unbelievable feats to gain their wants. Good measures of happiness are a logical end result.

A London newspaper asked the question, "Who are the happiest people on earth?" Four prize-winning answers were:

A craftsman or artist whistling over a job well done.

A little child building sand castles.

A mother, after a busy day, bathing her baby.

A doctor performed a dangerous operation saving a human life.

There were no millionaires among the winners. Riches and rank, no matter how the world strives for them, do not necessarily make happy lives.

Compassion for people is a reflection of mutual trust.

Develop a Caring Attitude

Do you care about many people?

Include all those people you encounter in activities outside the home such as on the job, in social and church functions. Perhaps you could count those you care about on the fingers of two hands! For many the fingers of one hand would suffice.

The world is full of lonesome people. Consequently there are many low achievers. Age, status, possessions, and wealth are no criteria. They exist in busy families, orphanages, among the aged, sick, and needy. They are especially prevalent among the vast labor forces of every nation. The top person of virtually every organization and government sits on a lonely pinnacle surrounded by difficult subjects awaiting decision. People in responsible roles among all occupations feel a sense of loneliness knowing their decisions affect lives, influence trust and confidence. Many people turn to unions to negotiate their needs and personal security—another reflection of trust and caring. Former President Harry Truman typified the loneliness of his powerful position with a sign on his desk which read, "The Buck Stops Here."

"People do not care how much you know, but they know how much you care" is an oft repeated phrase. It serves to convey the feeling one senses when a trusting relationship exists. Consider the messages and actions of some of the great names in history. For example, Abraham Lincoln, Franklin Roosevelt, Winston Churchill, Martin Luther King. When they spoke or took action, the listener felt a sense of trust and confidence in their message. Thus, it becomes apparent that the bond which cements people relationships is one of mutual trust anchored in a caring attitude. Can you develop a caring attitude? Yes, take heart; it can be done, but it must begin with you.

Mutual trust implies that each person has trust in the other. Trust is a relationship that is earned by actions and deeds. It is a reflection of one's sincerity, integrity, and honesty. A phony image or approach is easily detected. An air of honesty is unmistakable.

One of the great examples of building a solid and lasting attitude of caring is unfolded in the challenging experience of Herbert J. Taylor. He gave up a prestigious position of success to become president of Club Aluminum in Chicago, then a bankrupt company over $400,000 in debt. If it went out of business, 250 people would have lost their jobs. He said, "To win our way out of this situation, we must be morally and ethically strong. I knew that in right there was might. I felt that if we could get our employees to think right, they would do right. We needed some sort of ethical yardstick that everybody in the company could memorize and apply to what we thought, said, and did in our relations with others." Taylor later confessed that when such weighty problems fell in his lap, he would ask the Lord for help. Through prayer, twenty-four words came to him. The words served to guide Club Aluminum to recovery. Subsequently, Herbert Taylor served as the fiftieth president of Rotary International and his twenty-four word message was adopted by Rotary. Other associations have since used Herbert Taylor's message. Literally thousands have been influenced by what he referred to as, "The Four-Way Test." Here are the twenty-four words:

1. Is it the truth?
2. Is it fair to all concerned?
3. Will it build goodwill and better relationships?
4. Will it be beneficial to all concerned?

The four-way test is as valid and powerful today as it was when Herbert Taylor first recorded the words in response to his prayer for help. These words have changed the lives of many. Memorize them for yourself. Adopt and apply this four-way test to all things you think, say, and do. You will discover a genuine caring attitude for people is unfolding.

"In right there is might." Honesty, fairness, goodwill, and better relationships, plus sharing the benefits of your actions with people will add immeasurable strength to your AQ.

Compassion for people grows as rapidly as you demonstrate a caring attitude.

Be a Worthy Model

Do you consider yourself a model to follow?

Are you a model of initiative and leadership, enthusiasm, self-control, pleasing personality, willing worker, conscientious planner, tolerance, unselfishness, and mindful of other's needs?

While these and other characteristics might portray a model person, admittedly, few can be all things to all people.

However, every generation has its models. They may not be called models per se, but they reflect an image that people hold in awe, in respect. They may be comprised of students, housewives, athletes, actors, and people from all walks of life. Virtually everyone will respond when asked, "Who is your favorite statesman, actor, athlete?" Replies depict personalities that portray our own favored characteristics. Invariably these personal heroes reflect two strong qualities. These are self-respect and self-confidence.

Your achievement quotient rises or falls according to the degree of respect and confidence that associates have in you. It is simply the way you come through to others or "how people see you." In turn, your image to others identifies quite clearly how you feel about yourself, that is, your self-respect and self-confidence. People see you as you are, not as you may wish to be. It is evident that people need each other to be achievers in any field. Hence, heroes or models have the greatest following. They lead life's parade of people.

Self-respect is based on the same principles as respect for others. The comedian, Rodney Dangerfield, has built his career on the theme, "I get no respect from people." His routine develops a sequence of humorous examples of people showing lack of respect, much as seen in everyday life. "They laughed when I fell on the ice; even the ice made some bad cracks. I get no self-respect," says Rodney. He depicts an expression of disappointment, sadness, and depression, which invariably provokes lack of respect by others. And so it is in life. The image of self-respect comes from within.

Self-confidence is a companion of self-respect. Throughout the ages philosophers, psychologists, every champion and successful people in business echo the same thoughts. "You cannot be competent at anything until you first think you can be." This does not imply that you will achieve if you simply think you can. It does say that you cannot be a high achiever unless you believe deeply in yourself and your innate ability to excel.

To be a worthy model start by forming a good opinion of yourself and then deserve the good opinion of others. Here are ten steps to help build an image of self-respect and self-confidence:

1. Develop a deep consciousness of life's values. You were a miracle of life at the onset. Build on this value.
2. Write down your specific goals, timetables; expand knowledge and total awareness in your field of interest through constant study, exposure, and practice.
3. Build a positive attitude of expectancy, then demonstrate it with specific deeds and action for others.
4. Reaffirm your intent and needs by daily affirmations to yourself.
5. Establish a pattern of daily growth. Do something each day to earn respect and confidence.
6. Believe deeply in yourself and your ability to achieve.
7. Get involved with others and build a solid relationship of mutual trust and friendship.
8. Get excited about your potential achievement quotient and measure the progress.
9. Set your sights on the horizon just beyond your goal and plan to keep building for the future.
10. Look ahead, not back. Stand tall, not slouched. Walk with confidence, not despair. Smile at people, don't frown. Erect stepping stones, not stumbling blocks. Learn from setbacks, but never quit.

Compassion for people is the hallmark of a worthy model.

Motivate Others to Excel

Do people respond willingly to your guidance? If so, "humanity power" is serving you well. If not, do not dismay. Motivating others to perform assigned jobs, getting involved in their own development or taking action roles in community projects is a significant problem worldwide. Declining productivity levels throughout industry is a measure of the problem.

The word "motivation" tends to provoke mystery because it identifies with a universal problem. Theories, extensive studies, and books are numerous. For the purpose of this book, I shall focus briefly on some of the key factors that influence people response.

Motivation is a human act; it comes from within. Lilburn S. Barksdale, president of the Barksdale Foundation, Idyllwild, California, writes, "Let us look behind motivation. When we do so it is apparent that every human act is a response to a personal need or desire. Our basic need is to be comfortable, physically, mentally, and emotionally. Thus, our fundamental motivation, in a total sense, is to 'feel good' or at least to feel as good as the existing conditions will allow."(P. 14, *Building Self-Esteem by Lilburn S. Barksdale,* copyright 1972.)

Frederick Herzberg, distinguished psychologist, in a study of some 200 engineers and accountants working for eleven different companies, listed six key factors of motivation. They were personal growth, achievement, recognition, advancement, responsibility, and work itself. When these factors are listed in order of probable occurrence, it is apparent that good feelings would result. For example, work and responsibility denote involvement. This permits a person to achieve. In turn, recognition of results occur. This influences personal growth and advancement. The end result is good feelings.

Now consider a definition of motivation written by Louis A. Allen, author and consultant. "Motivation is the effort put forth by a leader to inspire, encourage and sometimes impel people to take action." Allen says, "To inspire is to infuse a spirit of willingness—people are inspired consciously or unconsciously, by a leader's personality, examples, and accomplishments. To encourage is to stimulate people to do what has to be done through praise, approval, and help. To impel is to force or incite action by any necessary means, including coercion and fear, if required. Further, that people are different in view of heredity, experiences; people are the same by reason of physical makeup and hierarchy of psychological needs." Thus, people respond to different forms of motivation.

Great achievers such as those in sports, business, government, and other roles are usually said to be highly motivated. They excel because of the satisfaction derived from the work itself, also because the work fulfills their apparent needs. Low achievers may not be deriving job satisfaction, enjoying the working conditions or circumstances in which they are engaged.

What then can you do to motivate others to excel? First, it is essential that you be motivated before endeavoring to motivate others. Your actions must demonstrate positive emotions, confidence in your judgment and ability. There should be an obvious compelling interest in the job as well as for the people being led. Picture the role of a coach in any sport. The job of training and building a winning team would be fruitless if the coach displayed negative emotions or was not motivated to excel or infuse players with a winning spirit.

Second, the essence of motivation in a total sense is to "feel good" considering human needs and conditions. Therefore, it becomes evident that you must reflect good feelings and, at the same time, generate good feelings in those who perform the job. It may not always be expedient to create good feelings, especially when the work at hand is undesirable. Justification of the need to do the work will tend to diminish the lack of motivation or desire.

Personal experience in management and sales activities throughout business and industry reveals that motivation is most effective when you: First teach or show people how to do what you want them to do, then guide as necessary. Second, give them freedom and responsibility to perform. Third, continually help them to feel good about themselves and their efforts. The noted German poet, Goethe, puts this with amazing relevance: "Treat people as though they were what they ought to be and you will help them become what they are capable of being."

Compassion for people radiates good feelings.

Walk in the Other Fellow's Moccasins

Do you listen to others' experiences and needs?
People are motivated to help or follow the person who (1) respects and uses the experiences of others (2) is sensitive to the reinforcement of others' needs. A significant reference is found in the adage from Indian lore: "Never judge another's needs until you have walked a mile in his moccasins."

It is often said that "experience is the best teacher" and it is true. But the cost of trial and error learning through personal experience is high and a slow process in today's rapidly changing environment. There is a better way! Use the experiences of others and you will find that the cost and learning time is greatly reduced. You quickly learn from the mistakes others have made; you discover more efficient and better techniques—time consuming wheel spinning is avoided.

I have known people with very limited education that rose to top positions in their fields. How did they do it? They took advantage of other peoples experiences and built on the best approaches. Too, they expanded their awareness through study and reading. This does not imply that you should forego formal education. Just be wise enough to draw on the efforts of others.

For instance, the average laborer, technician, manager, housewife, or neighbor often possess the experience you need. Invariably they will respond to the quest "I need your help." When this occurs and results flow, your learning cycle is shortened and the opportunity to raise your achievement level is increased.

It is one thing to use others' experiences for personal benefit, but is quite another issue to be responsive to their needs. Bringing other people into your confidence and using their knowledge and skills involves them in your life. When this happens a bond of mutual trust is established. The result of such involvement brings to the surface the most funda-mental need of all people—the need to feel important—to be recognized. Such needs are quickly and easily met when you extend compliments, thanks, recognition or appreciation for their help.

Recognition of others' input should not be overlooked or left to some future date. People who have responded to the request for help and established mutual trust will continue to aid and be supportive as long as they are credited or recognized for such aid. However, the warmth of a trusting relationship quickly turns cold if the giver feels they are being used or that you are taking credit for their ideas. To overcome this circumstance always give credit where credit is due; the giver will then be even more generous and anxious to help in the future.

Putting yourself in the other persons shoes opens wide a reservoir of talent and abilities to draw on—far beyond your own. You have immediate access to their total aware-ness; your learning time cycle is shortened; new resources for assistance are discovered; relationships are strengthened; new channels of opportunity are opened as your circle of friendship expands. And as you enlarge your sources of awareness your achievement level rises because others are helping.

As you apply the above philosophy, don't overlook the fact that you must buy your way in life. Not in a material sense—the achiever pays in sincerity, warmth, inspiration, and recognition of others' help. The value of walking in the other fellow's moccasins is vividly portrayed in the lines from an unknown author:

> It's easy to sit in the sunshine
> And talk to the man in the shade.
> It's easy to sit in a well made boat

And tell others just where to wade.
It's easy to tell the toiler
How best to carry his pack,
But you'll never know the weight of the load
Until the pack is on your back.

Compassion for people stimulates recognition of those who carry the load.

Help People Help Themselves

Do you willingly offer to help people in need?

"What do we live for, if it is not to make life less difficult to each other?" asked George Eliot. What a big difference there is between giving advice and lending a hand.

Some people cross the road or make believe they do not see an incident to avoid helping others. The news media frequently reports helpless victims were unable to attract help—people did not want to get involved. There are many who will only respond to a request for help when asked. They prefer not to volunteer; it may be fear of competition for their ideas. Then there are those who go out of their way to extend help, always aiding, sharing, teaching, or inspiring. They are often called "good samaritans." This particular group usually carries another label called "achievers." They have discovered that no one can climb the ladder of genuine success without taking others along.

A story is told of a man seeking to improve his communications ability because of poor grammar and the fear of talking to groups. He found a chapter of an organization called Toastmasters that sponsors member clubs where participants can study communication and leadership. Each member must develop speeches using well-structured educational manuals, then present them in a club setting for members to evaluate. This man soon discovered that he was receiving willing help from others for the development of his talents. What an opportunity, he thought. In a brief period he found he too was helping others develop their talents.

This man soon realized that an endless cycle of human development was in process. He saw the opportunity to help expand this picture worldwide. Advisors told him to get involved at the leadership level and help guide the organization. A personal creed evolved—it was framed in devotion to "Helping people help themselves develop their talents so they, in turn, could help others."

His efforts to help others and outgive members led, in ten years, to the role of International President of Toastmasters in 1978-1979. A portion of his creed, "Helping People Help Themselves" was adopted for the organization's annual theme. The organization now serves people in over forty-seven nations and has helped over one and one half million people raise their achievement quotient.

What an opportunity! What an achievement level, considering his start as a fearful communicator. It occurred as a result of helping people help themselves. The story is true. I know. I was that man.

Compassion for people harmonizes relations that enrich mankind.

Here are the basic points in this chapter, together with apothegms for reference:

1. Your world is a continual association with people. These associations represent the building blocks of personal achievement and happiness.
2. Humanity power is a result of the seeds you plant in life. Plant selectively, cultivate carefully, harvest with deep concern for people.
3. Attitude toward life in general and people in particular determines the height of achievement. The primary ingredient in a pleasant, productive attitude is harmony.
4. Self-concern is an obstacle to achievement. Focus your concern on others to gain needed cooperation and raise your AQ.
5. Accurate self-assessment identifies the strengths and weaknesses in your humanity power to influence those around

you. Two major forces are at work—emotion and logic. To act or react is your decision.

6. All people have a need to achieve. You need people to help you achieve. They need you.
7. People do not care how much you know, but they know how much you care. Apply the four-way test to what you think, say and do in relation with others.
8. Respect and confidence are values set by others based on your relationship with them.
9. Motivation is a human act; it comes from within. The essence of motivation is to "feel good" considering human needs and conditions.
10. Credibility is enhanced when you can speak from common experience or when drawing on the experience of others. Remember to always extend recognition to those who aid or assist.
11. Willingness to help others is a true samaritan image of humanity power.

APOTHEGMS

1. *Compassion for people adds meaning to your life.*
2. *Compassion for people is a gauge of attitude.*
3. *Compassion for people softens the voice of self-concern.*
4. *Compassion for people stimulates continual assessment of personal motives.*
5. *Compassion for people is a reflection of mutual trust.*
6. *Compassion for people grows as rapidly as you demonstrate a caring attitude.*
7. *Compassion for people is the hallmark of a worthy model.*
8. *Compassion for people radiates good feelings.*
9. *Compassion for people stimulates recognition of those who carry the load.*
10. *Compassion for people harmonizes relations that enrich mankind.*

2
Mind Power

There are but two powers in the world, the sword and the mind. In the long run the sword is always beaten by the mind.

—Napoleon Bonaparte

(PREPARATION)

This chapter is the exciting start of visits to six ports of call along the journey of PREPARATION. It is the first of three factors in the AQ formula multiplier. Preparation is as basic to achievement as the foundation of a ship's hull is to an ocean going vessel. The building of a ship and the pursuit of a goal starts in the same channel, the mind.

Could you place a value on your mental bank account?

The human mind is like a checking account. So long as you keep putting enough money in the bank, your checkbook is the most magic book in the world. All you have to do is pull out your pen, scribble your name, and the check becomes the password to your heart's desires. But stop making deposits, and the magic fades. The bank is quick to advise "insufficient funds."

Centuries ago, Solomon wrote, "For as a man thinketh

in his heart, so is he." Years later, Ralph Waldo Emerson stated, "A man is what he thinks about all day long." Great minds of the past and present may disagree on many things, but on this one thought there is unanimous agreement.

Modern psychology says: A man is what his creative mind says he is. You are not a body with a mind, but the reverse. You are a mind with a body. Mind is the power source from which all thought, character and action evolve.

"As the plant springs from, and could not be without the seed, so every act of a man springs from the hidden seeds of thought, and could not have appeared without them. This applies equally to those acts called 'spontaneous' and 'unpremeditated' as to those which are deliberately executed."

"Act is the blossom of thought, and joy and suffering are its fruits; thus does a man garner in the sweet and bitter fruitage of his own husbandry," wrote James Allen in his classic book, *As A Man Thinketh.*

Discover Your Power Reservoir

Do you enjoy peace, happiness, the riches of life?

Answering that question is a quick "yes" for many. For others, they might say, "Who would not like to have all these things in abundance?" Many do not realize there is a power in their possession which permits them to keep their mental bank account filled with sufficient strength to satisfy all their wants.

An acquaintance, Basile Johnson, gave up farming, sold out his equipment, and moved to a small neighboring town. There he took a job in the warehouse of a small plant owned by a major company. Basile's ability was soon recognized and promotions led him to the role of supervisor. In due time, the company offered Basile a job as warehouse superintendent in a sister plant located in the heart of a major city. He accepted the job and went to the city to locate a home. Not having spent time in a major city before, he was overwhelmed with the traffic, miles of buildings, congestion, commuter trains, and buses. In a few days he phoned the employer and resigned, saying he had decided to return to farming.

In the search for farm land and new equipment, he quickly discovered that prices of land and machinery had risen beyond his means. Distraught with worry and jobless, his wife Ann encouraged him to go back to the employer and tell him the real story. The big city was not for you and you quit of your own choice. He did. His work record was so outstanding and the employer was pleased to have Basile back on the job in the small community.

Basile chose to accept a position in the city. He then chose to quit his job. Then he chose to return to farming. Ultimately, he chose to return to his former employer. Four major choices were made that influenced the life of Basile Johnson and his family. He was exercising the greatest power source possessed by all mankind—THE POWER TO CHOOSE.

"Yes, you have this power, regardless of your religious beliefs. You choose the shoes, the car, the radio program, the vacation, the mate. You have this power. There was nothing outside of yourself to force you to make the decision that you did. You did it, because you made this choice. You made this choice because you wanted it so," wrote J. Martin Kohe in his book, *Your Greatest Power*. (Copyright, 1953, Combined Registry Company, published by The Ralston Publishing Company.)

Your power reservoir is thoughts. The depth is as great as your total awareness. This includes all of your knowledge and experience; it is everything to which you have been exposed. Your thoughts flow like water out of a bottomless well from within your mind. Thoughts of the past have molded your present status, conditions, and environment. Thoughts of today and tomorrow will determine your destiny.

Consider again that mental bank account. The thoughts

which you can withdraw from that account must come from such deposits as knowledge, skill, training, and experience credited to the account. Today's possessions have been processed through your account and the computer printer has issued a balance. Are you satisfied with the results? The choice is yours.

Preparation is the touchstone of achievement.

Develop Your Talents and Abilities

Is your self-development on-going?

Yes! would be the logical answer. Education, training, personal development is not something that is done for you. It represents what you do for yourself to develop your innate talents and powers. While various academic programs provide the curriculum and environment, the problem of one's development is left entirely to the individual. If you have made the decision to obtain certain qualifications for a field of endeavor, and to constantly update these requisites, then you have made a wise decision indeed.

Many people feel they have been short changed in education and training. As a result their job level is affected. They are being passed over by those who chose to seek higher academic credentials or specific skill development. Often those who feel deprived of education believe circumstance dealt them an unfortunate blow.

"Circumstance does not make the man; it reveals him to himself. No such conditions can exist as descending into vice and its attendant sufferings apart from vicious inclinations, or ascending into virtue and its pure happiness without the continued cultivation of virtuous aspirations; and man, therefore, as the Lord and master of thought, is the maker of himself, the shaper and author of environment. The divinity that shapes our ends is in ourselves; it is our very self," advocated psychologist James Allen.

An extensive study to identify some of the principles of

self-development was carried out by a major corporation, together with a team of psychologists, academicians, and consultants. Here are the key principles that were listed:

- All development is self-development.
  The effort must come from within the individual.
- Development is highly individual.
  The needs and desires of people vary.
- Development results from experience.
  Personal growth follows mastery of each task.
- Education is a continuous process.
  Obsolescence of education and experience occurs rapidly in our changing technical and social environment.

People can only function within the limits of their total awareness, that is, total knowledge, experience and exposure. For example, one who has not learned to fly a spacecraft cannot climb aboard and pilot the craft. The cabinetmaker and seamstress acquire awareness of their craft over an extended period of knowledge and skill development. Therefore, to move your achievement quotient to a higher level, it is essential to raise your total awareness level. It simply takes more to do more.

The first logical step for raising one's awareness level and, in turn, achievement level is to make a judicious assessment of the requirements to fulfill your goals. The procedure would be very much like planning a vacation. For example, your first vacation consideration would probably be "Where am I going—to what city, resort, beach?" Once that destination or goal is established you would proceed to plan—studying books, maps, literature, discussing your ideas with friends who have taken similar trips. Ultimately you would fix a schedule, the method of travel, budget the costs and consider all details so as to gain maximum benefit from the vacation.

The pursuit of self-development follows the same steps as planning a vacation. If you seek more education, a specific job opportunity, promotion to a better job or other activity, start by assessing the qualifications for the role. Then use your greatest power, that of choice. Decide on the merits of extending your awareness through additional education, training and experience to meet your goal. Follow this decision with a fully developed plan using the same criteria as in planning a vacation.

One of the characteristics of today's world is the increasing emphasis on knowledge and skill development to keep pace with changes and innovations in all phases of society. To assure survival in this rapidly changing, highly competitive environment, it is essential to continuously increase and update your total awareness level.

The road to higher achievement level is open to anyone with visions of the future, a desire to work, determination to succeed and a willingness to be patient until goals are reached. Set your plan for self-development in motion, then work your plan to assure fulfillment.

Preparation turns the revolving door of opportunity.

Think, Believe and Achieve

Do you think thoughts of achievement?

Your power reservoir and awareness of self-development principles have opened up a diamond mine of possibilities. The potential to reach new heights of achievement is just beginning to unfurl. However, there is only one way to get diamonds out of a mine. You've got to dig for them. The diamonds of thought are just below the surface waiting for you to uncover, process, polish, and market them. These precious gems of thought will not float to the surface to await plucking. They must first be imagined and identified. The worthy ones can then be mined with confidence, cut to shape, polished in the crucible of thought, then marketed.

"Whatever the mind of man can conceive and believe, it can achieve," wrote Napoleon Hill in his book, *Think and Grow Rich* (copyright 1963, Napoleon Hill Foundation, published by Fawcett Crest). The fruits of genius are usually a result of constructive thinking, savored in deep belief and pursued with serious intent of crossing the goal line. Constructive thinking can serve as a catalyst that will unleash a series of beneficial results. Therefore, ask yourself: "What do I think?" Are you thinking success or failure, positive or negative results? If the thoughts are negative you will not find any diamonds. You are simply kicking the dirt around. If the thoughts are positive you are ready to start digging for the gems and riches of life.

William James, noted psychologist, wrote, "Compared with what we ought to be, we are only half awake. Our fires are damped, our drafts are checked. We are making use of only a small part of our possible mental and physical resources." Some researchers have indicated we use only about 10 percent of our mental faculties. Think of the untapped capacity. Are you ready to put more of that reserve power to use? If so, put on your mining attire, pick up a shovel, and let's start digging.

The initial step is usually the hardest because it is higher than many are willing to step. It's labeled desire and that rhymes with higher, the starting point of all achievement. The great football coach, Vince Lombardi, equated desire power with mental toughness, then proved it—not once, but three times with three consecutive NFL championships.

"Mediocrity is self-inflicted and genius is self-bestowed," maintained Walter Russell. Desire power is self-inflicted.

It is said that "people never taste who always drink; people always talk who never think." Take time to think. It is the source of power. Believe in yourself. It leads to achievement.

> We live in deeds, not years; in thoughts not breaths;
> In feelings, not figures on a dial,
> We should count time by heart-throbs.
>   He most lives
> Who thinks most, feels the noblest, acts the best.
>   —Philip James Bailey

Preparation surmounts absence of thought and fortifies presence of mind.

Build a Character Image of Success

Are you satisfied with your character image?

I dare you to think great thoughts about yourself. The real purpose of books is to influence readers to do their own thinking. It is my fondest wish that as you read these and other pages you will be inspired and exicted to think deeply about yourself and the things you want to accomplish. I encourage you to think big thoughts about your potential. Make no little plans. Think of big plans. They can be cut to suit the ultimate need, if necessary. As the Texan said in response to a query about his exaggerations, "I don't really lie, I just think big."

President John F. Kennedy said in a historic address to Congress on May 25, 1961, "I believe that this nation should commit itself to achieving the goal, before this decade is out, of landing a man on the moon and returning him safely to Earth." The goal was achieved with man's first walk on the moon in July, 1969. Big thoughts evolved big plans. The result was a big achievement.

The nature of your thoughts shapes the character you will build. Character grows out of deliberate choices between what you should do or might like to do. Thoughts of character are like a collection of bricks piled up day by day and ultimately cemented together with the mortar of habit. Without realizing it, we form the house of character in which we live, for good or ill.

Some people tend to build their character image like playing a round of golf. As soon as they get out of one hole they head for another. And sand traps are strategically placed to catch the bad shots. Thomas Dreier has given us a pointed picture: "No lions are ever caught in mouse traps. To catch lions, you must think in terms of lions, not in terms of mice. Your mind is always creating traps of one kind or another and what you catch depends on the thinking you do. Your thinking attracts you to what you receive."

Building or rebuilding a desired character image of success

will not occur overnight. But it can be done. Such changes are founded in thoughts and molded in desire. It takes time, patience, consistency of thought, and action. A person lays the foundation of true greatness when he becomes more concerned with his character image than expanding his reputation. C. D. Boardman put it concisely:

> Sow a thought, reap a habit;
> Sow a habit, reap a character,
> Sow a character, reap a destiny.

Here is a sequence of steps to consider for the process of building or rebuilding a character image of your choosing:

1. Picture clearly the character image desired and the changes you wish to achieve.
2. Assess your strengths such as talents, abilities, gifts; also determine the weaknesses to be overcome.
3. Write down the steps necessary to polish your strengths for maximum growth; also the requirements to upgrade specific weaknesses. Endeavor to keep those notes in pocket or purse size cards, say 3" x 5", for easy day-to-day reference. Establish dates to accomplish each step. Then put your plan into action and keep notes on progress.
4. Review your needs list several times daily.
5. Read good books related to your needs. Seek professional counsel as necessary.
6. See yourself becoming the person you want to be.

Preparation forges habits of good character and tempers soundness of thought.

Tune in Your Subconscious

Are you in tune with your habitual thoughts?

Mind is the great lever of all things. Habit patterns are easily formed, often without awareness. They are like invisible seeds planted in the fertile loam of thought and produce both good and bad results.

One of the most popular musicals in recent years was, "My Fair Lady." It is based on the play *Pygmalion* by George Bernard Shaw. His plays were usually written about heroes and heroines in many walks of life who pulled up their roots, who moved ahead, that the race might follow.

The will that drove them forward was not always their own. They seemed to be in the iron grip of a mysterious power that Shaw called the life force. *Pygmalion* depicted this unseen life force. The legendary story portrays a sculptor in Greek mythology who carved a statue in marble of a beautiful woman. So perfect was it that he fell in love with his creation, adorned it with flowers and jewels, spent days in devoted admiration, and Venus gave life to the statue. The play centers on the education of Eliza Doolittle, a cockney flower girl and how Professor Henry Higgins, the life force, turned her into an elegant lady.

There is more than pagan mythology to this story. Scientists have concluded the concept is more than a visionary idea. Any person can set before the mind's eye the image he would like to be, and then breathe life into it merely by keeping that image before the subconscious mind as a model on which to build. This phenomenon is called "self-fulfilling" prophecy. People tend to become what they prophesy for themselves.

The 1929 stock market crash was said to have been influenced not so much by economic conditions as by the attitudes of people aroused by the prophets of doom who envisioned financial tragedy.

Numerous studies have been made that support the self-fulfilling prophesy. A hundred military cadets were randomly assigned to one of five math classes. Instructors were advised that the students were divided according to levels of ability. Those in high ability classes improved their math substantially.

The coach who expects his team to win has a better win

record than the one who reflects doubt. Psychologists are employed by numerous professional teams in football, baseball, basketball, and other sports. Why? Professional counseling helps to mold a positive attitude toward achievement, to be as great as talents and awareness allow. "Our chief aim in life is somebody who shall make us do what we can," advocated Emerson.

I am intrigued to watch musicians, jazz, and others, who can play by the hour without one reference to music. Of course they, like many professionals in other fields, have had years of practice. But reflect on the thousands of motions you make daily without deliberate thought. The mental system of control is comparable in both instances. Practice forms habit patterns that can be repeated without thinking.

The subconscious mind serves like a computer system, classifying and storing data flowing from the five senses. It controls the body functions, the heartbeat, blood flow, and provides direction for mending and maintenance functions. Personnel in the computer field say that if you put garbage or wrong data into the system, it will produce only garbage. They refer to this as GIGO—garbage in, garbage out. A good example of GIGO in the subconscious is the common language habits of many who constantly use meaningless word fillers like "ya know," "I mean," "in terms of," plus numerous "andas," "uh-huhs." All are habit patterns planted in the memory storage banks of the subconscious that flow freely without thought.

One of the best ways to reach and use this power is to impress upon the subconscious the things you want it to do or act upon. That is, plant the seeds of the model or preferred habits and then act upon them as though you were in the role. It is a universal law that all power but one, Divine power, is both positive and negative. This law is applicable to the subconscious. Therefore, be optimistic, pursue positive thoughts and avoid negative emotional reactions. When innuendos such as fear, jealousy, greed, revenge, and anger strike you turn toward positive emotions of desire, hope, love, and enthusiasm. The subconscious mind, an incredible mental computer, will classify and process the data you put into it. Remember GIGO. Build habit patterns that you can tune to for growth and achievement.

> Thought in the mind has made us.
> What we are by thought was wrought and built.
> If a man's mind hath evil thoughts, pain comes on
> him as comes
> The wheel the ox behind. If one endure
> In purity of thought, joy follows him
> As his own shadow, sure.
>
> —James Allen

Preparation arouses thoughts in the fathoms of the subconscious mind.

Let's now consider the main points of the chapter and the apothegms:

1. The human mind serves like a bank account for deposits and disbursements of knowledge and experience.
2. Your mind is a reservoir of unlimited power. It sustains your greatest power—the power of choice.
3. All development is self-development. Only you can set the pace—it's your choice.
4. You can be whatever you choose to be. Growth starts with aspiring thoughts, followed by a deeply seated belief in yourself to be an achiever.
5. Character is shaped by the nature of your thoughts. It grows out of a deliberate thinking pattern. Dare yourself to think great thoughts.
6. The subconscious mind is a source of unrealized power. It serves much like a computer processing data. Remember GIGO, garbage in, garbage out.

APOTHEGMS

1. *Preparation is the touchstone of achievement.*
2. *Preparation turns the revolving door of opportunity.*

3. *Preparation surmounts absence of thought and fortifies presence of mind.*
4. *Preparation forges habits of good character and tempers soundness of thought.*
5. *Preparation arouses thoughts in the fathoms of the subconscious mind.*

3
Want Power

*Ask, and it shall be given to you; seek
and you shall find; knock and it shall
be opened unto you.*
—Matthew 7:7–8

(PREPARATION)

Are your wants clearly defined?

That perhaps sounds like a silly question, but it is very significant. It is said that the primary difference between what one has and what one wants is a problem. And problems that are well defined are usually half solved. Therefore, when wants are clearly defined, spelled out in detail, formed into goals and plans, the wheels for achievement can be set in motion. If this is not done there is a strong probability the want will turn out to be nothing more than an emotional reaction or whim.

Many decisions stem from emotional responses. Business and industry leaders often make emotional decisions in spite of well-developed plans. When this happens the entire system of setting objectives, budgets, or plans falls apart. The results can be good or bad. Well-thought-out action plans have usually proven the best course to follow.

The benefits of defining wants in detail are numerous.

Foremost is the elimination of spur-of-the-moment mistakes. Big decisions such as those covering the purchase of a home or a car, or when one uses a high ratio of borrowed money, require careful evaluation to avoid incurring debts beyond one's means. Credit financing of virtually any consumer item and many services is common practice today. Frequently, buyers find themselves unknowingly taking on debts beyond their means. This forces the irrational buyer to exist from one payday to the next.

Wants are a serious consideration. These soon become a mental fixation and remain so until satisfied. Frequently wants are identified with something tangible, an object, or a person. People go to great extremes to satisfy their wants. Examples abound of those who live beyond their means; some resort to crime, nations go to war. The power of such human force, often founded in emotions, exceeds the imagination. Consider the emotions of love, enthusiasm, hope, jealousy, hatred, revenge, greed, and anger. Each such emotion emits power of great consequence.

This chapter is devoted to the techniques of harnessing the tremendous energy in want power. When controlled and put into constructive goals and action plans, the results will have an impact of great proportion on your achievement quotient.

Analyze Your Problems

Do you attempt to satisfy specific needs?

I indicated herein that the primary difference between what one has and what one wants is a problem. There is a human tendency to go after wants without consideration of needs. For example, in our young married life, Helen and I solved our housing requirements by renting an apartment. We really wanted a house and knew that want would be satisfied in due time. But at that moment we needed shelter, and the apartment would suffice. Too, we needed transportation to travel to and from work, for shopping and to pursue the usual interests of urban living. We really wanted a new car, but settled for a used one. It satisfied our needs of that moment and matched our financial picture. Ultimately, we would find a way to satisfy our want for a new car.

The basic approach to a want problem is to first determine the magnitude of your problem. That is, endeavor to separate emotions at the outset and focus on needs. The real purpose for this consideration is to reduce the emotional bias that most wants are founded upon. It also helps to reduce those spur-of-the-moment mistakes that sometimes drain the bank account. The stress of such mistakes tends to lead to other emotional reactions such as second source financing to ease an immediate burden. Extreme reaction and unrest over unwanted burdens can lead to catastrophic decisions like quitting a job, divorce, and similar calamities.

Analysis of your problem serves to eliminate reactionary measures and helps formulate well-thought-out solutions. It may sound complex and time consuming, but when viewed as a logical process your decision will be more rational and satisfying.

How can you improve your batting average in solving want or need problems?

Here is a simple logical sequence:

1. Write out the problems. This is done to reduce the words to paper so they can be thoughtfully considered. The mere effort of writing forces one to search for words that clarify what the problem really is. Too, this provides thought time to eliminate some of the natural bias of needs vs wants. Try to focus on needs at first. These may or may not be the same as wants.
2. Gather together all the available information on the conditions or circumstances of what you have and those of the object you want.
3. Consider alternatives. These would be the different ways of satisfying the problem.

39

4. Weigh the alternatives against your definition of the problem. Each alternative should be assessed as to the degree it satisfies the problem. For example, the problem may be one of relocating to a larger home to accommodate an expanding family. Houses vary in size, location, and cost. Which satisfies the problem in keeping with financial considerations? The problem may be a particular educational program. Choices may include in-state and out-of-state schools. Which satisfies the problem and fulfills the need?

5. Choose the best alternative. Then consider the future adverse consequences that may occur as a result of your choice. This serves to force reconsideration of costs, long-range gains, and similar factors.

6. Make your final decision after thoroughly examining all factors. The odds are in favor that your decision will be a sound one. The unforeseen mistakes of a reaction approach to problems will have been eliminated.

Preparation stimulates logical action and eliminates illogical reaction.

Set Definite Goals

Are you pursuing well-defined goals?

In the story *Alice in Wonderland* there is an interesting exchange as Alice asks directions from the Cheshire Cat, "Would you tell me, please, which way I ought to go from here?" asks Alice. "That depends a good deal on where you want to go; if you don't know where you are going any road will take you there," said the cat.

The message is clear. The road to failure is paved with good intentions. Many have the right aim in life, but fail to pull the trigger. Achievement is usually a result of setting specific goals supported by well-thought-out plans, pursued with the intent of reaching a specific point at a predetermined

40

time. Plans stem from personal or organizational goals. Results accrue to those who constantly seek goal progress and follow it step by step to a successful conclusion. Thus, goal setting and goal seeking activities become companions of achievement.

I consider goal seeking one of the most important functions of an achiever regardless of the activity. To set goals is important, but goal seeking focuses on achieving specific results. Keeping one's eye on a picture of the expected end results creates a mental image of fulfillment before the event actually occurs.

Goal setting should be considered for any short- or long-range endeavors that warrant your time. This would include personal development, job search, home and occupational projects. Goal setting stimulates the adoption of a plan and without that "any road will take you there."

Frank Bettger in his book *How I Raised Myself from Failure to Success in Selling* (copyright 1949, published by Prentice-Hall, Inc.), writes about the results achieved in organizing work. "I set aside Saturday morning and called it self-organization day. Did this plan help me? Listen! Each Monday morning, when I started out, instead of having to drive myself to make calls, I walked in to see men with confidence and enthusiasm. I was eager and anxious to see them because I had thought about them, studied the situation, and had some ideas I believed might be of value to them. At the end of the week, instead of feeling exhausted and discouraged, I actually felt exhilarated and on fire with the excitement that next week I could do even better. It is surprising how much I can get done when I take enough time for planning, and it is perfectly amazing how little I get done without it."

To achieve goals, I find that a guidance system helps to keep projects on track. The successful landing of man on the moon was achieved through the intricacies of a complex guidance system. The same philosophy pays off in achieving satisfactory goal results.

The guidance system I use involves a procedure that I remember by relating each step to a letter in the acronym GOALS. It will serve an individual or a group effort. Here's how it works:

- GATHER the data needed to pursue the goal—marketing information, materials, manpower, money.
- ORGANIZE people and/or functions for specific parts of the project.
- ACT to provide guidance, time targets, checkpoints and control for each phase; keep wheels in motion.
- LINK activities of all participants to a common communications network. Make the process of reaching the goal a team effort.
- SEEK frequent status checks, always painting a daily sequential picture focusing on expected end results.

Goal setting and thoughtful planning will put you on the track for achievement. Goal seeking will keep your plans on track providing you use a good guidance system.

An inscription on Hopkins Memorial Steps, Williams College, Williamstown, Massachusetts reads:

> Climb high
> Climb far
> Your goal the sky
> Your aim the stars

Preparation framed around specific goals and plans influences favorable results.

Develop Action Plans

Are your goals supported by well-thought-out plans?

Perhaps you have discovered that wishing consumes as much energy as planning! Successful businesses today build day-to-day and future activities around detailed plans. Planning is the offspring of objectives and goals established by key managers and leaders. Good plans serve to stabilize any organization's continuing ability to compete in the world marketplace and prosper. The same philosophy applies to individuals. To be an effective achiever, one's personal and job objectives or goals must be supported with good planning.

It is said that a vast majority of people die relatively poor, but with music in their hearts. Songs that were never sung, not because their intentions were not right, but because their plans were not right. As an exercise, try listing the names of 100 people born in the same year, then trace their levels of achievement. Less than 15 percent will have risen to top positions and wealth.

Developing an action plan for your objectives or goals is simply organizing the effort required in a systematic and constructive manner. Many allow their lives to flounder and succumb to plans developed by others to lead them. Welfare ranks high as an example. It provides for many who, for whatever reason, have no plans. Economics of the average U.S. household revolves around credit purchases. Many purchases such as homes with mortgage financing are sound investment plans. But many smaller purchases are influenced by clever advertising to arouse human emotions to buy. Emotional purchases are seldom made to satisfy a well-thought-out plan.

Action plans to support your objectives and goals can be quite simple. I discovered that a complete and easy plan can be derived by following Rudyard Kipling's famous adage: "I have six honest serving men. They taught me all I know. Their names are WHY, WHAT, HOW, WHO, WHERE, WHEN." Here's the way it works:

WHY —Describe purpose of the plan or project.
WHAT —Write the goal or objective based on the purpose.

43

HOW —List methods or steps to accomplish the "what," include money source as a step.

WHO —Assign people to be accountable for the various steps; include follow-up reports, cost control.

WHERE—Identify arrangements or location.

WHEN —Assign time frames and schedules for each step and for the total job or project.

I suggest you develop a simple form to include these six steps. Then it is easy to fill in the blanks with proper information. You will find that well-thought-out plans are a useful tool for any project. They serve to organize effort.

Obstacles sometimes occur in the best laid plans. This often happens when one loses sight of the goal. But most such stumbling blocks can be resolved by rerouting the methods. The six-step plan makes it relatively easy to reroute around obstacles. "What can't be cured must be endured," is a worthy maxim when facing the unsolvable. Just keep your mind on the goals and action plans will bring immeasurable dividends.

Preparation of written plans converts senseless meandering into sensible action.

Share Your Goals and Plans

Do you possess stick-to-itiveness?

People often set goals with good intentions, then file them in a desk drawer or in their mental filing cabinet. When that piece of paper or brilliant idea is out of sight the thought power which stimulated it begins to fade. What may have been a worthy goal is reduced to a faint wish. No action or effort will be put forth. Ultimately, the wish also fades and other thoughts take its place.

The adage "two minds are better than one" is a reality. You are limited in the thought process to the sum of your total conditioning in life including heritage, knowledge, experience, exposure, and intuition. When others are brought into your goals and plans, the circle of total awareness is expanded. "Our most valuable possessions are those which can be shared without lessening—those which, when shared, multiply. Our least valuable possessions, on the other hand, are those which, when divided, are diminished," wrote William H. Danforth in the book *I Dare You* (copyright, 1969, by the American Youth Foundation).

In his twenty year study of great leaders, Napoleon Hill revealed that Henry Ford began his business career under the handicap of poverty, illiteracy, and ignorance. Within ten years he mastered the handicaps and in twenty years became one of America's richest men. Further that his most rapid strides became noticeable from the time he became a friend of Thomas Edison. Later he formed the acquaintances of Harvey Firestone, John Burroughs, and Luther Burbank. With these brilliant minds in the picture consider how much Henry Ford's circle of awareness was expanded.

I believe you too can benefit from sharing your goals and plans with one or more people where mutual trust exists. This may be a relative, friend, or associate. Be cautious to confide only in those you believe will think with you in a positive way. As in everything, the negative mind can shatter your fondest dreams. Negative thinkers seldom have constructive ideas or goals because their thought process concentrates on destruction, not on building.

Sharing your personal goals with a small circle of trusted acquaintances tends to stimulate confidence. Intelligent, positive thinkers can contribute guidance, help overcome obstacles, avoid wheel spinning, and reinventing things that may already exist or failed for some reason. Another great advantage of sharing with carefully chosen people is that it tends to provide reinforcement. This, in turn, lights an emotional spark of persistence to keep your thoughts on track.

You, of course, are the originator of personal goals. If your plans do not materialize or if the persons with whom you have shared become negative, then regroup and rebuild. As your revised plan takes shape select other confidants. Many great ideas fall by the wayside when thoughtless negativism enters the picture. The closer a confidant, the greater the impact of negative thoughts. Don't be discouraged. If the goal was worthy at the outset it must be worthwhile to persist. Don't hesitate to revamp and commence again.

Thomas Edison dreamed of inventing a lamp that could be operated electrically. It is said that he failed ten thousand times until his dream was realized. If you are on a good track and believe the result will be fruitful, persist. Edison later said, "Seventy-five percent of the world's failures wouldn't have failed at all if they had only kept at what they were trying to do. Our greatest weakness," he said, "lies in giving up. The most certain way to succeed is always to try just one more time."

Sharing goals and plans is not a new concept. But some feel a bit insecure in discussing their goals—they view them as secrets. The founding fathers of the American form of government sought to insure freedom and democracy by writing it into the Constitution of the United States and structuring three principle components of government. Each would be dependent on the other for success of their endeavors. These are the executive, judiciary, and legislative branches. While government is a far-flung entity that harbors few secrets, except for national security purposes, the concept of three branches serves to foster sharing and, in turn, the intended safeguards. In similar manner the sharing of goals and plans will serve to fortify your thoughts, solidify direction, sort the wheat from the chaff, and keep the schemes on track to fruition.

> Never give up! If adversity presses,
> Providence wisely has mingled the cup.
> And the best counsel in all your distresses
> Is the stout watch-word, Never give up!
> —Samual Glover

Preparation for the pursuit of goals and plans is reinforced when shared.

Plant Seeds of Expectancy

Is your outlook one of happy anticipation?

You probably know one or more people who simply bubble with happy anticipation of results. They radiate an aura of excitement that many would like to emulate. Those people who tend to reflect a bright happy outlook on daily events are usually found among the achievers. They have discovered that a confident, joyous approach to life's problems has a big payoff—favorable results.

An in-depth study of patterns in management of several hundred executives revealed three dominant types or styles: autocratic, democratic, catalytic. The autocratic is fairly well described by the word—dominant-forceful. Democratic tends to lean toward self-direction and control, and is permissive. However, the catalytic type is a more favored style in that this manager arouses the will in others to achieve. You see, the catalytic type is an aroused person, is expectant, anticipates results and can stimulate others by example.

"Your life is what your thoughts make it," wrote the Roman Emperor, Marcus Aurelius. It is just as easy to implant thoughts of success in your mind as it is those of failure. Most people at one time or another have experienced victory in some manner, sports, on the job, and in school. Invariably when winners are asked about their accomplishments you will hear or read the expression "I knew I could." When you live in an attitude of expectancy, many of the petty problems seem to melt away. When you expect the best, that's what you receive.

Goals and action plans stand the best chance of being fulfilled when one expects the best results. The power of expectancy stems from seeds of positive thought planted and nurtured in the mind. Expect the best at all times. Then if you have to hurdle a few tough obstacles, you will have generated the strength and courage to do so. In fact, seeds of expectancy seem to arouse emotions of confidence making it fun just to figure out how to surmount obstacles. Solving difficult problems can be half the fun of pursuing a goal. It is said that true enjoyment is in pursuing something, not in catching it. Expectancy generates excitement and enjoyment follows.

William E. Henley as a young man suffered from tuberculosis of the bone. He had operation after operation, including the amputation of one foot. His health gradually deteriorated and doctors told him that he had only a short time to live. Sitting on a hospital bed and pondering his fate, he wrote these words:

> It matters not how straight the gate,
> How charged with punishments the scroll,
> I am the master of my fate;
> I am the captain of my soul.

Henley lived another thirty years. He planted and cultivated the seeds of expectancy and went on to live a fruitful life.

Problem solving, goal setting and seeking, developing action plans to achieve your ambitions should be undertaken with thoughts of expectancy. Therein lies the joy of becoming successful and raising your achievement quotient.

Preparation kindles the spark of expectancy for achievement.

Recapping the key thoughts in this chapter, remember:

1. Wants are a serious consideration. They carry both helpful and destructive power. Assess them thoughtfully.
2. The difference in what one has and what one wants is a problem. Resolve problems in a constructive way by following six simple analysis steps. It will pay good dividends.
3. Goal setting and goal seeking are paramount to obtaining the results you want when you want them.
4. Action plans should contain all the tools for keeping your goals on track. Follow Rudyard Kipling's six honest serving men. They are Why, What, How, Who, Where, When.

5. Two minds are better than one. Expand your total awareness by sharing goals and plans with trusting confidants. Regroup and rebuild as necessary. Never give up.
6. An attitude of expectancy fosters a positive outlook to obtain desired results. Goals and action plans stand the best chance of being achieved when you expect the best results.

APOTHEGMS

1. *Preparation stimulates logical action and eliminates illogical reaction.*
2. *Preparation framed around specific goals and plans influences favorable results.*
3. *Preparation of written plans converts senseless meandering into sensible action.*
4. *Preparation for the pursuit of goals and plans is reinforced when shared.*
5. *Preparation kindles the spark of expectancy for achievement.*

4
Imagery Power

In order to see it is not sufficient merely to open the eyes. There must be an act of the mind.
—Francois Millet

(PREPARATION)

Do you see images of your goals?

The power to portray a mental picture of potential results is not a phenomenon. It is an intelligent application of thought and concentration. The successful architect envisions in the mind's eye the picture of the skyscraper before putting lines on paper. The successful artist envisions a landscape before applying brush to canvas. The successful stage performer envisions an audience and anticipates their reaction before the curtain opens. Successful people endeavor to apply imaginative powers to current goals and long-range plans. They picture end results and resolve problems along the way to reach a predetermined point.

"Every man takes the limit of his own field of vision for the limits of the world," said Arthur Schopenhauer. The majority of people who follow the same routines day after day settle into a mold of contentment. Having seen and felt the same environment over an extended period the motivation to look up, look out, look ahead is dampened. Their imagery power is dormant. Contentment has settled in the mind. Memory and imagination fade due to lack of use. If one desires "apathy can be overcome by enthusiasm, and enthusiasm can be aroused by two things: first, an ideal which takes the imagination by storm, and second, a definite intelligible plan for carrying that ideal into practice," suggested Arnold Toynbee.

There is nothing that can prevent you from picturing images of your goals, plans, and desires. You have infinite power in your mind which, when utilized, renders such force that other material things around you are insignificant. Marcus Aurelius, the Roman Emperor, offers an appropriate thought: "Live as on a mountain." Envision the heights you want to achieve are at mountaintop. You will be inspired to soar as high as your view of the end results. A simple statement which Omar Khayyám recorded has permanent wisdom: "Heaven is but the vision of fulfilled desire. And Hell the shadow from a soul on fire."

Visualize what you want in your mind. Mentally picture what your goals and plans will look like when completed. The pictures should be so detailed that you can actually see yourself possessing the item, making the sale. If it is a college degree you are after and the years of study ahead cast a spell of drudgery, envision the graduation ceremony, how you will look in cap and gown, your relatives in the audience, the thrill of receiving your diploma. A mountaintop vision will cause you to reach for new heights and dispel feelings of despair. If it is a meeting you will conduct, visualize the room, people in attendance, picture success and harmony, also people congratulating you on a successful program.

Now examine the current and future goals, plans, and desires on your plate and ask yourself: "Can I see clearly the end result?" If so, begin to enjoy the trip. If not, find a mountain-top and paint realistic mental pictures. Eliminate stumbling blocks—mold stepping stones along a pathway to achieving your dreams.

See Yourself Becoming

Does personal growth match your dreams?

To become what you are capable of becoming represents progress and growth. To be just as you are indicates a stalemate in the rapidly changing world if no effort is made to keep abreast of events.

All progress and growth is a matter of change. The first characteristic of life everywhere is change, growth to modifying circumstances and events. But it is the responsibility of the individual to control and direct those changes necessary to achieve personal growth to become and not just to be.

The future belongs to things that grow whether it be a person, a tree, social custom, or democracy. Our primary concern should be to do better today than we did yesterday. Longfellow's "Psalm of Life" expresses it in verse:

> Not enjoyment and not sorrow
> Is our destined end or way,
> But to act that each tomorrow
> Finds us further than today.
>
> Let us then be up and doing
> With a heart for any fate,
> Still achieving, still pursuing
> Learn to labor and to wait.

One of the interesting aspects of the extensive motivational studies conducted by the late Dr. Abraham Maslow was his focus on outstanding psychological specimens. He chose this approach in contrast to some psychologists who based their research on animals, the ill and those classed as average individuals. Maslow compared his approach to that of the athletes who studied the best performers as a means of improving their own. The higher achievers, according to Maslow, were self-actualizers in that they maximized their talents and abilities. It is apparent that this type of individual seeks to become and not just to be. In other words, the outstanding performer is fulfilling one of the suggested definitions of success stated in the introduction, that is, "optimizing one's God-given talents."

The law of growth is a step-by-step process. In order to activate a program that leads to achievement, there are four elementary steps that must be satisfied.

1. You really gotta wanna. The choice of direction and application of one's talents must be fully committed to the venture. Half-hearted interest is essentially the same as no interest. Without commitment there will be no worthwhile action.

2. Write out the goal and prepare an action plan. Specify dates for completion of each step. I have emphasized before and will repeat again and again, reduce your goal and action plan to writing. This action forces you to think through a logical step-by-step sequence of things to do.

3. See yourself becoming. Visualize the role you really want and paint a mental picture of how you will look and act when the pinnacle is reached.

4. Display a strong spirit of interest and enthusiasm. Nothing is accomplished without these vital ingredients. The spirit of interest will show in your face; enthusiasm in your action.

With these fundamental steps working for you, nothing will impede your progress and growth. However, no one achieves great heights by their own efforts unless they do two things. First, commit themselves to the role being pursued. Second, do something about it each day, no matter how minor the gain. Small gains daily add up to big measures in due time. Constantly keep in view the mental picture of the goal or end results desired; see yourself becoming. It will add inspiration to keep you moving forward step by step.

As you move forward always be mindful of the people, past, present, and future who play a role in your achievement. "We should so live and labor in our time that what came to us as a seed may go to the next generation as blossoms, and that what came to us as a blossom may go to them as fruit," recommended Henry Ward Beecher.

Preparation with a vision of end results adds realism to growth.

Control Input and Output

Do you control your thinking?

To optimize one's talents and abilities, to turn in the best possible performance, it is necessary that thoughts be controlled. Your mental thought process can be controlled. It regulates the input and output of information and action. Alternatively, it will control you when left to the flow of emotional distractions and impulses.

Life is a game in a sense. It can be challenging, rewarding, fun or one of boredom, disappointments and unhappiness. We sit at the control panel and direct or accept the course of our travels. Game winners are usually average people who have a faculty for applying what we call common sense. There is always reason for good or bad results. Some search for the magic that leads to good results; some accept what comes and call it fate. But for every good effect there will be a cause. In the game of life there is no substitute for clarity of purpose supported by well-defined goals and action plans. These tools become the luxury of controlled efforts.

Two significant factors come into play when a conscious effort is made to regulate input and output. They are the laws of desire and habit. Desire or wants are strong emotional forces that dictate response. Desires are best fulfilled when a well-defined picture of the object is held in the mind, then reduced to paper for clarity. Emotional force will react and accomplish the desire. Therefore, the chances of success are greatly enhanced and the time element reduced, when accuracy of the plan is on paper. In other words, with a plan in view, accurate thought can be controlled.

Habit grows out of doing the same thing in the same

way over and over again until it becomes repetitious without deliberate thought. Habit is the basis for memory training as demonstrated by the many deeply engrained actions performed daily—driving on familiar routes, remembering names, faces, places, and a myriad of numbers. Habit grows out of environment. Thus, it is important to be selective about the environment since this is the source of seeds for mental growth from which decisions are made. These two factors, desire and habit, serve as a mental filtering process that needs careful control to influence your achievement quotient.

Mental discipline is a key to mastering control of actions. Man is impulsive by nature and this leads to irrational decisions. An impulsive action can cause disastrous consequences such as occurred on an airplane. A passenger, without thinking, responded to an impulse to pull the red handle on an emergency exit door. Pressure pulled the door out and passengers were momentarily in a state of panic. Fortunately, all had their seat belts fastened and, flying at low altitude, the plane was able to land without serious injury to anyone. Most people react on impulse on occasions. Who hasn't responded on impulse to a "wet paint" sign by sticking their finger in it just to see if it really is wet.

The mind does not serve as an effective filter unless a conscious effort is made to program it through deliberate thought and the elimination of impulses. It requires tuning out a mass of extraneous messages such as gossip that clutters thought. While this is not always easy, it is practical to be selective about sources of information. Small talk, spending excessive time with nonproductive people fills the mind with nonproductive messages that interfere with controlled thought.

Thomas Edison, after becoming a telegrapher, discovered his deafness did not prevent him from hearing the clicking of the telegraph. He became an excellent operator because the distractions were tuned out. Once he told Edward Marshall he was glad to be shut off from small talk, saying he did not hear conversation at the boarding house dining tables where he ate. "Freedom from such talk gave me an opportunity to think out my problems. Things I have needed to hear, I have heard," he indicated.

Ability to control the flow of information to and from the mind is a discipline that requires practicing. Desire and habit are primary forces for effective concentration. A healthy mind is one free of negative emotions. I recommend the adoption of a personal creed that spells out your intended life style. Commit it to memory. Then repeat it daily to yourself. It will serve as a constant reminder of the difference between right and wrong approach to motives.

Here is my personal creed; it has served me well. Don't hesitate to use it or simply write one that suits your needs.

MY CREED

To pursue life with integrity, honesty, patience and sincerity; to love God, my family, my fellow man, and my role in life; to be a creator of circumstance through realistic goals and plans; to work with diligence of purpose; to deliberately think about and continuously develop my physical, mental, social, and spiritual resources; to read selectively of good books and writings; to build meaningful friendships; to dream of higher pinnacles on distant mountains; to unselfishly help others develop their talents; to laugh at my own mistakes; to be satisfied with nothing less than my best effort in all things and, when each task is completed to remain unsatisfied.

Preparation refines thought and controls output.

Bury Negative Thoughts

Do you pursue life with a positive outlook?

Imagery power is like a dead battery when negative thoughts are present. A story from the *American Salesman* told of a woman who was on tour of a thriving Bible camp and came across a small burial ground. Her guide said, "The camp you see today might not have existed without this cemetery." He explained, "In the early days, when the camp was a dream, somebody was always saying 'if we had the money we'd build,' or 'we can't build now,' or 'it's impossible to go ahead!' We were stymied until we came up with a dramatic idea for getting rid of our stumbling blocks. We buried them." The visitor took a closer look at the gravestones. "Here lie words that hinder," said one, and on the other three were carved the words, "if," "can't," and "impossible."

So you see it is possible to get rid of negative thoughts. Bury them. Growth and progress occur as a result of planting and cultivating positive thought and action. It is like planting good seeds in fertile soil—with care you can expect a good crop. But plant the best seeds in clay and growth will not occur. To further portray the effects of our emotions, consider the following emotions and probable reaction:

POSITIVE EMOTION

Desire —start of achievement; aspiration to reach out.
Faith —optimism, trust and confidence.
Enthusiasm —excitement and eagerness to move forward.
Love —happy display of good feelings.
Hope —expectation, anticipation, looking ahead.

NEGATIVE EMOTION

Fear —anxiety, apprehension, distrust, agitation.
Hate —strong dislike, avoidance, unfriendly.
Jealousy —resentful, envious, suspicious.
Greed —selfish, lustful, seeking self-satisfaction.
Revenge —wanting to inflict injury, to retaliate.

It becomes obvious that little can be accomplished when the mind is absorbed with negative thoughts. Fortunately, the mind does not deal with positive and negative thoughts at the same time. One or the other will dominate. Thus, a person is in complete control. The power of choice comes to the surface and only the person in charge can activate the hot button of decision.

In some instances, negative emotions dominate because the person has an overdeveloped sense of perfection. This leads to setting standards beyond their talents and abilities. Accomplishment falls short of their standards and the person says, "Oh, what's the use—it's impossible." There is nothing wrong with setting high standards, but when it continuously results in feelings of failure, it is time to adjust the procedures or standards. Failure should not be viewed as the end; it simply means success is yet to be achieved and the effort may require smaller steps to reach the goal.

When I am faced with very difficult tasks and the standards seem beyond my immediate reach I apply the "swiss cheese" approach. I start with the view that the mass of the project is like a big block of solid cheese. Since it is too large to consume in one bite, I begin to punch holes by doing small bits at a time. In a short period I can see that the big block of solid cheese is showing many holes. In due time when the project is completed it will resemble a big block of swiss cheese, full of small holes. Do not hesitate to cut projects down to size if the magnitude leads to negativism. Keep avoiding thoughts of "can't," "impossible," and replace them with those of "I can," "I will," and "patience."

During World War II, the army adopted a slogan, "the difficult we do immediately—the impossible will take a little longer." It became a by-line for thousands and served to bury negative thoughts and supplant with seeds of positive action.

Faith, a positive emotion, is an invaluable resource power. It sees the invisible, believes the incredible, and receives the impossible. With strong faith it is difficult to say what is impossible, for the dreams of yesterday are the hope of today and the reality of tomorrow. Use this resource power and stay on a positive track to raise your achievement quotient. You too can achieve the impossible. Grow with faith as your guide.

Preparation filters out negative factors that impair progress.

Take off the Blinders

Are you aware of the world around you?

Imagery power is influenced by the degree of total awareness in those things going on around you; people, activities, community, state, national, and international issues and events. These factors shape the environment from which growth occurs. It takes a curious active mind and broad vision to stay abreast of daily events and changes. Since these are the basis for attitude and outlook on life it is important to stay informed. Ideas and acceptance by others are viewed on how they harmonize with present and future environment.

In horse racing, blinders, which are two leather flaps, are intentionally fastened to the horse's bridle to keep it from seeing to the sides. The horse's sight is purposely held to the track ahead to avoid distractions. The average person is blessed with peripheral vision which is that area of vision lying just outside the direct line of sight. This faculty permits a person to observe a wide portion of the landscape and surrounding activities. The function compares with the wide angle lens of a camera. It can be adjusted to focus on a wide or narrow expanse. It is said that over twenty percent of the people do not use their peripheral vision paying little attention to people and activities around them. Shyness and lack of confidence are often factors of influence. It is as though they were wearing blinders. Unfortunately, their awareness is limited to the pathway ahead much as the race horse. The horse's vision is deliberately guided, whereas the individual can take off the imaginary blinders and greatly expand his awareness.

Being aware and informed is tantamount with growth primarily because these are the bases of communication strength. For example, a manager who does not keep up with economic forces, human relations elements, such as equal employment rights, safety and health regulations, is headed for problems. Communications with others is an indispensable ingredient for growth. Hence, the broader one's vision, the better one's understanding of the environment.

As a teacher and counselor in public speaking, I often encounter timid personalities who have great difficulty in making eye contact with an audience. Their eyes focus on the floor, walls, and ceiling. Until the student can overcome this problem and make personal contact with individuals and the total audience a message falls flat. There is no feeling or understanding between the speaker and the audience. The speaker is simply talking to himself.

The ability to generate conversation and, in turn, achieve understanding is stimulated by eye contact. Expression and interest are not only expanded when looking into the eyes of another person, response is more spirited, there is a greater sensitivity to feelings and awareness. Conversation is more friendly and is less likely to be misunderstood. Sparkling and attentive eyes are a reflection of sincere interest.

Therefore, enhance your imagery power and your achievement opportunities by looking into the eyes of people, looking ahead and to the sides taking in the total world in view. Cast off the blinders, if they exist, and seek to expand your visual awareness.

Preparation opens the eyes to new horizons.

Dress for Where You are Going

Are you aware that attire depicts your values?

A look in the mirror at morning before facing the outside world may feedback a silent response, "I like myself—I look and smell good enough for today," or "the shirt/blouse worn yesterday is a bit soiled, but it will do for today," or "there wasn't enough time to shower, but who cares?" A book is known by its cover. And so it is with man's appearance. Outer clothing covers about ninety-five percent of the body, thus carries an unspoken message of significance.

The image portrayed through clothing and appearance for any function such as work, sports and social activities generates many decisions among viewers. Therefore, it is timely to ask: "Are you dressed for the role you are in or the one depicted in your long-range goals?"

William Thourlby in his book, *You Are What You Wear* (copyright 1978, by William Thourlby, published by Sheed, Andrews and McMeel, Inc.), states that "when you step into a room even though no one in that room knows you or has seen you before, they will make ten decisions about you based solely on your appearance. They may make many more, but you can be assured they will at least make the following. Your:

1. Economic level
2. Education level
3. Trustworthiness
4. Social position
5. Level of sophistication

6. Economic heritage
7. Social heritage
8. Educational heritage
9. Success
10. Moral character"

Since attire does depict image then it should definitely portray the confidence and stature of the role described in your long range goals. In other words, dress for where you are going, not where you are. Of course, common sense must prevail for each working environment in which you are situated. An engineer working in a mine or factory who expects to be the top manager in time would obviously dress for the day-to-day working conditions. When attending meetings or functions outside the mine or factory, then clothing should be worn that is suited to the occasion. Whatever the environment or occasion may be, it should be noted that there is no substitute for cleanliness. While clothing may cover many body deficiencies, it will not conceal aroma; powder on top of unbathed bodies only accentuates. Keep in mind that your image power should be apparent to the viewers' eyes, not their noses.

Selection of suitable colors, quality fabrics and current styles are important to your image. Look closely at the attire of most movie characters and you will note that designers endeavor to place emphasis on the performer, not on their clothing. Business and industry leaders today are using clothing counselors for guidance both for themselves and employees representing their organization to the public. A deliberate effort is made to improve their overall image through the appearance of employee representatives. Political figures, including the presidents, have used clothing advisers. It was particularly evident that Presidents Nixon, Ford, and Carter turned to conservative suits and ties after taking office with intent of focusing the viewers' eyes on themselves and not on their clothing. Bright flashy colors have their place and are enjoyable to look at, but in business and many other circles, they detract from the individual and may depict an unwanted image.

Some interesting surveys have been done by clothing counselors, designers, and writers. John T. Molloy refers to one he did in his book, *Dress for Success* (copyright, 1975, by John T. Molloy and Thomas Humber, published by Peter H. Wyden) which points out job classification tends to indicate color choice. For example, he states a beige raincoat is generally worn by members of the upper-middle class and black raincoat in the lower-middle class. The expression "you are what you wear" does reflect meaning.

While clothing choice and dress is very much a personal matter, it represents the manner in which you choose to market your talents and abilities. Clothing is the outer wrapper of the product you are marketing. Quality of the package content is portrayed by the outer wrapper. Go for quality attire rather than quantity, just as you would in purchasing a car, furniture, or other commodity. It will not only serve you longer but will definitely provide a better image as you seek higher achievement plateaus. As in any sales promotion, the presentation of a product to a potential buyer is all important. And people can be choosy. After all, when accepting the product they also get the style of packaging. To recap the key suggestions and help set the tone for building imagery power, remember:

1. Dress for where you are going, not where you are. The confidence stimulus is then carried in the mind and worn over the body.

2. Dress to keep the viewers' attention on your talent and abilities, not on what you are wearing.
3. Go for quality rather than quantity. Put a quality wrapper around a quality product.
4. Seek advice of a reputable clothing counselor. Read appropriate reference materials to maximize your image power with well-chosen attire for every occasion.

Preparation of a top quality product justifies a top quality wrapper.

A summary of chapter key points and the apothegms follow:

1. Picture clearly the end result of your goals, plans, and desires. Live as on a mountain and cut pathways leading to the top.
2. Progress and growth are a result of change. Picture yourself as you want to appear when goals are reached.
3. Adopt mental disciplines to master control of actions. Control the flow of information to and from your mind for achievement. Adopt a creed that describes your intended life style and build on it.
4. Bury the if's, can't's, and impossible's. Plant, cultivate and harvest positive growth-oriented thoughts.
5. Absorb the world around you to expand awareness and enhance your image. Remove the blinders that block your view.
6. Clothing covers about ninety-five percent of the body. Package yourself for success. Dress to match the intent of your long-range goals.

APOTHEGMS

1. *Preparation with a vision of end results adds realism to growth.*
2. *Preparation refines thought and controls output.*
3. *Preparation filters out negative factors that impair progress.*
4. *Preparation opens the eyes to new horizons.*
5. *Preparation of a top quality product justifies a top quality wrapper.*

5
Fitness Power

If you have built castles in the air, your work need not be lost; that is where they should be. Now put foundations under them.

—Henry David Thoreau

(PREPARATION)

Do you follow a balanced fitness program?

Two men were discussing the high rate of taxes and government waste of money. Just then a school bus passed by. "See what I mean," said one. "When I was a boy we walked three miles to school and three miles back home each day. Now we spend thousands of dollars for a bus to pick up the children so they don't have to walk. Then we spend a million dollars to build a gymnasium so they can get exercise." Life styles have indeed changed as has the environment for finding a quality of life that suits each person's needs. The search for the ideal environment and balanced life style seems never ending.

Fitness is a many faceted subject. It means different things to people. To many it is associated only with physical agility, stamina, and endurance. Life's ladder of achievement does depend on physical fitness. But the application of fitness power is much broader. It encompasses one's whole life style. When viewed in perspective it resembles the finite balance of perpetual motion. Achievement level therefore is equated with the pursuit of a balanced life style or total fitness, not merely physical fitness.

A sports magazine writer was interviewing a popular quarterback of a professional football team. The quarterback was noted for his passing ability and skillful field maneuvers, but sometimes his choice of words might be questionable. The writer, seeking to understand the player's philosophy, quoted a verse from the inspirational writings of Jack London:

> I would rather be ashes than dust,
> I would rather my spark go out as a burning flame
>   Than it be stiffled with dry rot.
> I would rather be a splendid meteor
>   Blazing across the sky,
> Every atom in me in magnificent glow,
> Than to be a sleepy and permanent planet.
> Life is to be lived, not to exist.
> I shall not waste my days trying to prolong them,
> I will use my time.

"What does that mean to you?" asked the writer. After pondering and thinking deeply the quarterback replied, "Throw deep." An apt choice of words and expressive philosophy. Go for the big one, go all out. The same rationale is applicable to total fitness. It represents a balanced approach. The key to competence in all sports is balance; the ability to match foot and arm movements with body position. Balance is also the key to a higher achievement quotient.

An interesting conversation by a group of admirers of a noted leader was in process. One said, "Joe looks and acts fit as a fiddle," another "Yes, and he is sharp as a tack," another voice said, "And isn't he enjoyable to be around?" and a fourth says, "His faith is as solid as a rock." The observers were identifying with a well-balanced life style, perhaps because it represented one they would like to emulate. Each comment spoke to a level of fitness. That is, physical fitness—fit as a fiddle. Mental fitness—sharp as a tack. Social fitness—enjoyable to be around. Spiritual fitness— rock-solid faith. The admiration added up to total fitness power. Quality of life and total fitness go hand in hand. To further explain how fitness power can work for you I am going to "throw deep" on each of five plays that follow. You are the receiver!

Go for Total Physical Fitness

Will physical fitness carry you over your goal line?

It is not uncommon for people to let their bodies get out of shape, overweight but undernourished, low resistance to disease, low respiratory capacity. When faced with problems or personal wants that exceed fitness level, a crash diet and exercising program is adopted. Then when the body is in shape, laziness or some other stimulus takes over and the body again reverts to poor shape. An endless cycle of shaping up and shaping down occurs. Most people go through this cycle. I am no exception.

At one time I was shaping down more than up. Then at forty pounds overweight I was advised that a gall bladder operation was essential. A large solid stone filled the bladder and infection could be serious. Hearing the doctor say "we must operate" was frightening. My reaction was to first get my body in shape. Since we seem to act quickly when a purpose exists, I sensed the need to avoid any medical complications due to neglect of my body. I asked the doctor, "How much time do I have to prepare for the operation?" "Why?" he asked. "Because I want to first get in better physical shape and take off my excess weight and build up my fitness with exercise," I responded. He agreed that while delay was risky, seven or eight weeks was acceptable. He offered to put me on a proper diet and recommend a series of exercises. The forty pounds came off and the stone mass came out successfully. A rapid recovery, according to the doctor, was attributed to fitness. The lesson was a lasting one. The purpose for getting in shape for an operation prevailed. As a result, I have maintained a continuing total fitness program of daily exercise, common sense nutrition, plus vitamin supplements. I can now wisely advise, don't wait for an emergency to justify your purpose.

Research has shown that a physically fit person has more endurance and stamina. He is better equipped to tolerate physical exercise; has a more efficient heart and greater lung capacity. Of great importance is a proven connection between mental alertness, absence of nervous tension and physical fitness.

To improve the quality of life you must feel good about yourself. Improving fitness improves appearance. A person who is out of shape creates a self-image that matches the shape—poor. It evidences a lack of concern about life, job, social and other activities. Why? Feelings about external things usually harmonize with internal feelings about one's self. Hence, body condition and self-image go together. Shape up the body and self-image will automatically shape up.

Wholesome physical activities and nutritional food are the basis for increasing life's values including longevity. In recent years many cities and communities have taken steps to provide more recreation facilities and educational fitness programs for all ages. One city receiving publicity for an all out effort is Hartford, Connecticut (*Prevention Magazine,* March 1979). The local planning commission structured a program to improve the quality of life for everyone that would take part. Schools, day-care centers, office and factory personnel, residents of rest homes and others joined the program. Fitness exercises were designed for each age and activity level.

A report of students taking the Kraus-Weber fitness test showed fifty-nine percent failure among boys and fifty-five percent among girls. In eight weeks the failure rate had dropped to forty-seven percent for boys and twenty-seven percent for girls. Teachers report that student discipline has improved, attention span is longer. The teachers also indicate they are less tired and that stress is down due to students' fitness and alertness.

The benefits of a sound fitness program are apparent. Significant is the fact that participants do feel good about the quality of life that results. This, in turn, affects performance levels and, of course, achievement levels.

There is no magic approach to total fitness. It is a personal problem. Each person must make a choice that best suits his needs. The first consideration always is to obtain a doctor's advice on the best approach to fitness based on current physical condition. A myriad of fitness programs are available to meet any need. It becomes a matter of selecting what is best for you, recognizing the value and then doing something about it.

A physical fitness program produces best results when pursued continuously. Total fitness requires total commitment. This eliminates the cycle of shape up, shape down. You deserve the best. To maximize your achievement potential give yourself the best in total fitness—shape up and keep in shape.

Preparation matches body fitness with goal posts.

Apply Common Sense Principles

Are you noted for using common sense?

This gem of advice, use your common sense, has been passed from generation to generation. It is the essence of mental fitness yet the simplistic thought inferred is often cast out in search of something more profound. Problems solved by ordinary common sense are many, varied in complexity and often of great consequence. Common sense is a measure of the possible. It represents normal intelligence, good judgment, intuition, understanding, presence of mind, shrewdness, balanced reasoning, wisdom, and unbiased impulse. It is a faculty possessed by most people, but its use is often substituted with irrational choices. "Common sense is only a modification of talent. Genius is an exaltation of it. The difference is, therefore, in degree, not nature," counseled Edward Bulwer. It is said too that "fine sense and exalted sense are not half as useful as common sense; he who would carry nothing but gold will always be at a loss for change."

A farmer was detained for questioning about an election scandal. "Did you sell your vote?" asked the attorney. "No sir, not me," protested the farmer. "I voted for the man because I liked him." The perturbed attorney said, "C'mon now, I have good evidence that the candidate gave you twenty dollars." "Well," the farmer said, "it's just plain common sense that when a man gives you twenty dollars you kinda like him." The rationale may be questionable, but it is an application of common sense.

"Knowledge without common sense is folly," advocated Nathaniel Lee; without method, it is waste; without kindness, it is favoritism; without religion, it is death. But with common sense, it is wisdom; with method, it is power; with charity, it is beneficence; with religion, it is virtue, and life and peace."

The principles of common sense are founded in knowledge and application generally follows one of several courses: for goals and objectives, personal and occupational, the starting point is purpose; for problems it is cause; for solutions it is effect.

A worthwhile goal or objective must be framed around a well-described purpose if it is to succeed. Research has clearly established that people need a purpose to achieve; they acquire direction through purpose and are therefore motivated when a need is identified. However, an ill-conceived purpose or one to which little thought has been given leads to floundering and disappointing results. When a worthy purpose or need is first reduced to a specific goal or objective and the method of achieving that goal clearly spelled out in an action plan, wisdom prevails. Knowledge will have been applied with methodology to obtain results.

Assume you plan to obtain higher academic credentials, say a master's degree in business by attending courses at night. Apply the first common sense step. Identify the purpose, write it in goal format, that is, "to achieve a master's degree in business in two years." Then write out an action plan following the steps outlined in Chapter 3 and pursue your need with good judgment. Thorough study and a constructive approach insure the chance of fulfillment.

Problems are usually a deviation from some norm or standard, say the car does not start, the dinner was late or the meat overcooked. These are problems and the failing was caused by human acts, mechanical faults or perhaps acts of nature. It is no disgrace to fail, but to do so intelligently the cause must be determined. In the words of Alexander Pope:

Judge not actions by their mere effect;
Drive to the center, and cause detect.
Great deeds from meanest springs may take their course,
And smallest virtues from a mighty source.

Resolve the problems by first identifying the deviation from standard and determine a sensible sequence of steps to correct. If, for example, the aforementioned master's degree program got off track, don't lose hope. Examine the action plan and assess the cause. Perhaps the time period was set too tightly or the job and extra activities do not allow adequate time for study. Once the cause is clearly assessed then modify your action plan. A well-established plan eliminates the guess work and contributes to sound reasoning.

Solutions to problems do not always work out as planned. Bear in mind that solutions are merely the effect that result from resolving the problem cause. If inadequate thought was given to the cause, a chosen solution may generate poor results. Again, consider the master's degree program. Lengthening the time period to obtain the degree may have solved the pressure so you could maintain several other activities. But, if it caused a year's delay in competing for a key job that required an MBA, then the solution to lengthen the time period was perhaps unwise.

Many of life's daily activities are pursued and resolved quickly and without the simple paper work I have referred to. However, if you consistently apply good common sense principles to purpose, problems, and solutions on major issues, then accuracy rate on smaller ones will be greatly increased. Your mental fitness will be apparent.

Preparation using common sense discloses genius.

Enjoy the Company of Others

Are you building social relationships?

To "build social relationships" is an apt phrase because that's the way it is. Relationships are dependent on the builder and not on the receiver. Virtually everything in life is dependent on people relationships and success in any role is dependent on the strength of such ties. This strength is referred to as social fitness. The politician is dependent on relationships for election support; the manager on subordinates for production results and customers for market support; the actor depends on the stage hands. Examples are manyfold. But it is the strength of confidence and mutual trust in relationships that spells stardom or failure.

Without friends in business and the community you would be classed as a total stranger. It becomes apparent that you need people to succeed in any endeavor, but people may not necessarily need you. Hence, building of relationships must start with the person needing an association with others. The only way to make a friend is by being one.

My family and I have enjoyed living and working in various parts of the world—several locations in the United States,

England, Europe, Middle East, Hong Kong, and Australia. While this is not an uncommon experience in our mobile society, each move meant building new relationships in business and the communities. It was sometimes difficult and trying. But always worthwhile in the end as lasting and cherished relationships were developed.

During the period of relocating to various places seven key factors served to solidify relationships and build rapport with people. They will work for you in building meaningful relationships, as well as mutual trust in family, business, and community life.

1. Turning on a warm personality. Three actions that stimulate good feelings at the outset are a firm handshake, a smile, and some comment of praise about the person, their home, office, or city. Such actions must be in good taste and not presented in a phony manner. You must reflect a genuine interest to be appreciated. This becomes very evident to the average person on first impression. You only have one opportunity to make a first impression.

2. Making people feel important. Everyone has an innate desire to feel important. This factor ranks among the most significant ways of opening the mind of the listener; it opens wide the door to mutual trust. Look for areas where a person's environment or accomplishments justify recognition and extend appropriate words of praise. Avoid false praise. It is quickly recognized and will close the listener's mind rather than open it.

3. Remembering names. You can not build confidence in others unless a tone of sincerity is evident in your voice. To remember a name is like magic—the respondent may be surprised and say, "Oh! you remembered my name." That is a compliment of confidence in you. Most say they can't remember names, but don't forget faces. The truth is they simply do not try. Remembering names is a process of association and repetition. Therefore, on introductions ask the new acquaintance to repeat his name. Try to associate it with a place or object, preferably a silly reference. For example, if the name was, say, Mike Cobb—see a micro-phone in the shape of a corncob hanging from his nose. Sounds ridiculous. It is meant to be. You will remember the silly picture and the name. Then, when you speak with the individual make frequent use of his name. Association and repetition will be your servants.

4. *Building confidence in others.* Confidence is the foun-dation of friendship. Neither money nor possessions will buy this relationship. It must be earned by establishing mu-tual trust and respect. This starts by showing interest in others rather than first trying to sell yourself, your products or wares. William James said, "The deepest principle in human nature is the craving to be appreciated." Showing interest in others tends to satisfy that feeling of being appreciated and becomes a basis for trust.

5. *Being a good listener.* No form of communication seems to receive less attention than listening, yet is a most powerful tool for building confident relationships. Research-ers say we spend 9 percent of our communication time writing, 16 percent reading, 30 percent speaking, and 45 percent listening. Thus 75 percent is spent talking or listen-ing. While many courses are offered in writing, reading, and speaking, it is only in recent years that much attention has been extended to listening techniques. To be a good listener you must develop an attitude of wanting to understand and appreciate the other person. It must include a willingness to dispel prejudices and give credit to a speaker. One little used technique is to listen with your eyes. This means looking intently into the eyes of the speaker. It enhances concentra-tion power on the speaker's words. Remember that a good listener earns mutual trust quickly, but also learns something about the speaker in the process.

6. *Pursuing win-win relationship.* Everyone wants to feel as though they are a winner or can hold their own in a conversation. Put-downs and shutting off opinions of others will not build happy relationships. It is all right to disagree, but do not be disagreeable. When others offer objectionable

opinions, a simple "Yes, I respect your views, but I believe such and so" will build rather than destroy relationships. Each person will feel he has won his point. Endeavor to let others feel they are not defeated—everyone has opinions and is entitled to be heard. Build mutual trust with a win-win approach.

7. *Being flexible.* There is great strength in flexibility. Few issues are either totally one color or another, rather shades of difference will exist. Being opinionated destroys confidence. Inflexibility frequently arises out of feelings of inferiority or immaturity, thus a person feels the need to prove himself. The person sees only one color, never shades in between. This inflexible attitude reflects obstinacy, not intellect. Whereas flexibility denotes confidence and good judgment. Do not settle for "humble pie" in resolving mistakes. Seek mutual trust by being flexible.

The joy of your life will be enhanced as you deliberately try and consciously seek to enjoy the company of others and build social fitness. Following the above seven steps will serve you in any endeavor; they are of particular value in sales activities. But that is really everyone's role, isn't it? Selling yourself, selling your talents, your abilities and your wares, and relationships with others.

Preparation reveals confidence and pleasure of people relationships.

Count Your Blessings

Are you drawing on the power of the universe?
An inventory of all your possessions will remind you of the power of the universe and the impact it has on your life. You started life as a miracle. Many gifts have come your way; talents, abilities, love of family, friends, freedom to think, act, and do. Count your blessings. They have come to you as a result of your belief. They represent your spiritual fitness. Believe in the limitless supply of God's goodness.

The universe is filled with more wonders than anyone could possibly conceive.

"Ah, but a man's reach should exceed his grasp. Or what's a heaven for?" These words by Robert Browning reflect man's unending desire to achieve. To reach one goal is satisfying momentarily. Then dissatisfaction occurs and a renewed challenge spurs man to reach for greater heights. The life force within is constantly being renewed as man moves ahead to reach new goals. The spark of this unseen life force is a result of thought from the depths of our mental bank. Thoughts are engendered from the seeds of one's personal development and spiritual strength—this strength comes as a result of belief, preparation, and total fitness. It represents balance in life.

Consider the strength of spiritual fitness through one's religion. "Religion does not occupy any one part of man's life. It is the reaction of a man's whole being to his object of highest loyalty. Religion must be felt and thought. It must be lived out; it must translate itself into action. Religion is not a segment of life, nor is it connected with any one time or place. It is not just a ritual, ceremony, doctrine, or the church, even though these may all be aids in stimulating it. The great religious leaders of the race have spoken of religion as a vital, personal experience. This experience grows out of real needs—the need for courage and companionship in life. Micah speaks of man's chief duty, 'To love mercy, to do justly, and to walk humbly with thy God.' For Jesus the great commandments were love of God and love of one's neighbor. Whether religion has been interpreted as man's cooperative quest for the values of life or as 'the spirit of God in the soul of man,' it has been stressed as involving the whole of life," reflected Harold H. Titus.

The power of the universe is on your side. To know that this infinite power is readily available for the asking is reassuring and the basis of hope. Where would we be without hope and faith? The frustrations and complexities of life baffle the mind. We often forget that simple faith and prayers have sustained men and women for thousands of years. While our capabilities and burdens have increased over the centuries, one thing has remained constant; the power of prayer.

In Alfred Tennyson's moving description of the dying King Arthur, the king tells the last of all his knights, Sir Bedivere:

Pray for my soul. More things are wrought by prayer
Than this world dreams of. Wherefor let thy voice
Rise like a fountain for me night and day.
For what are men better than sheep or goats
That nourish a blind life within the brain
If, knowing God, they lift not hands in prayer
Both for themselves and those who call them friend.

The miracle of America is based on prayer, for prayer begins where all miracles must begin, with the individual. Prayer enables us to look at other miracles of life, the people we deal with and to discover in each person something important and worthy. Our concern goes beyond ourselves to the other person—and that is important. Every person hungers for recognition, appreciation, admiration, and love.

The football player, Willie Davis, heard that his beloved coach, Vince Lombardi, lay dying in the Doctor's Hospital in Washington. He hopped on a plane in Los Angeles and on arrival in Washington went straight to Lombardi's bedside. He stood by the bedside only a few minutes; then left the hospital and boarded a return flight to Los Angeles. On arrival, reporters questioned Willie, asking, "Why did you do that? You flew twice across the United States just to stand for a couple of minutes in the presence of a man who probably didn't even know you were there." Willie said, "I had to. Because whenever I was with that man, he always made me feel like I was important. He always made me feel like a special person."

Count your many blessings and gifts. Especially the gift that enables you to share life with people, to make them feel like somebody and, in turn, feel like somebody, too. This brings about a vital balance in life.

Preparation exposes the blessings of life—talent, abilities, faith, hope, love.

Balance Your Style

Are your work and time available balanced?

It is easy to take on more work or community projects and find yourself overloaded. There are times when one must learn to say no. Yet, we find that high achievers in management and other roles can juggle many tasks with great efficiency. They have learned to delegate quickly when practical, choose reliable assistance as required and manage their time efficiently. The work load is kept in balance. They pursue a balanced style to keep from dropping the ball.

Mark Twain commented on this factor in a similar vein indicating "The miracle of the power that elevates the few is their industry, application, and perseverance, under the promptings of a brave, determined spirit." It is, I believe, the balance of these forces within that enables man to excel. It is the fitness of each source of man's energy that enables him to pursue a balanced style. A chain is as strong as its weakest link. Strengthen the weak link and the chain's overall capacity is increased. Ronald Arthur Hopewood's poem, "The Laws of the Navy," magnifies this thought:

> The strength of the ship is the service
> And the strength of the service, the ship
> On the strength of one link in the cable
> Dependeth the might of the chain:
> Who knows when thou mayest be tested?
> So live that thou bearest the strain.

The weak chain philosophy is applicable to the balance of one's life style. Raising the level of physical fitness tends to stimulate a greater work effort. You simply feel like doing more. As capacity for work increases so does the desire to learn how to achieve more, hence mental fitness is increased. An increase in mental awareness stimulates the desire to be more socially conversant with people because the range of interests are broadened; there is more to share. The blessings that evolve create a greater awareness of the unlimited spiritual power available and this channel is opened for continuous study. An endless cycle of ever increasing power evolves through fitness.

It is no secret that exercise of the body is essential for a healthy physical existence; that knowledge is the foundation of awareness; that social activity provides an array of pleasures; that spiritual strength is the bond of faith, hope, and love for all mankind. The secret to higher achievement is unknown and untried by many. It rests in the ability to deliberately and consciously build on each of these four sources of strength. Not just one, but all. The overly developed physical specimen is limited to an attractive body unless other faculties are developed. The overly educated person who places all value on intellect may not be able to find or hold a job suited to the education without a balance of interests. The playboy or playgirl may have a limited future by ignoring other life forces. The overly pious Christian reflects an image of sadness thinking others are out of step.

There is no substitute for total fitness. It is not a one time effort, rather an on-going activity that gives balance to life and your style.

Preparation demonstrates total fitness to pursue new opportunities.

Pertinent points in each section of the chapter and the apothegms are:

1. Total fitness as described herein includes the development and balance of physical, mental, social, and spiritual strengths. It encompasses all major resources which sustain the quality of life.

2. Wholesome, well-regulated physical activities are essential to good health. And when you have good health you have about everything. Feeling good about life sets the stage for achievement.
3. The principles of common sense reflect wisdom when applied. Remember they are threefold, namely: purpose to support goals and objectives; cause to cope with source of problems; effect to insure workable solutions.
4. Life's social barometer is based on the development of meaningful relationships with people.
5. Count your blessings often. It unlocks the thoughts of appreciation and stimulates words of praise to their source. The power of the universe is on your side. Ask, and it shall be given to you.
6. A chain is as strong as its weakest link. To maximize your achievement potential, strive for balance in your life style.

APOTHEGMS

1. *Preparation matches body fitness with goal posts.*
2. *Preparation using common sense discloses genius.*
3. *Preparation reveals confidence and pleasure of people relationships.*
4. *Preparation exposes the blessings of life—talent, abilities, faith, hope, love.*
5. *Preparation demonstrates total fitness to pursue new opportunities.*

6
Resource Power

*No army can withstand the strength
of an idea whose time has come.*
—Victor Hugo

(PREPARATION)

Do you use all your resources for achievement?
I have asked this personal question of many people. The typical responses are: "What do you mean?" "I think so," "I'm not sure," "I never thought about it." One person said, "I don't know—how many should I have?"

When most people consider this question, their thoughts immediately turn to financial strength, property owned, and other material possessions. While such assets do represent resources, aside from outright inheritances or gifts of money and property, these accrue as a result of putting forth one's personal efforts.

As we delve further into the process by which to increase the achievement quotient our concern is to focus on the resource powers that each person has available for self-development. These factors comprise the ingredients utilized in achievement.

No doubt the thought has crossed your mind that you really could be greater than you are. You may have considered expanding your knowledge through additional academic sources, or seeking a better job. There is no limit to the possibilities of expanding your potential. The Bible says, "you are heir to a kingdom." Plant that belief in your mind. It is literally true. You can be greater than you are.

Have you ever heard a person say, "I wish I knew how so and so can accomplish so much!" For outstanding achievers their many activities often appear effortless. My observation is they are not simply using brute force or exercising superior intellect. Rather they tend to utilize all their sources of strength in a more efficient and organized manner.

Thomas Jefferson was known for his versatility and great accomplishments. During the presidency of John F. Kennedy, a group of internationally known scientists was invited to the White House. The president told them they represented the greatest collection of talent in the world except when Thomas Jefferson was in the same room. He mentioned that Jefferson was a young man of thirty-two who could tie an artery, break a horse, calculate an eclipse, build an edifice, try a cause, play the violin, dance the minuet, and write the Declaration of Independence. Jefferson's versatility and daily accomplishments were evidence of great strength. While he had the same resources at his call as other people, it is apparent he applied them much more effectively than many. These same strengths are available to you. It is simply a matter of learning to apply them effectively to increase your achievement quotient.

Now let us magnify the effective use of these primary resources as discussed in the previous chapter. With awareness of the resources and how to use them, another vital link in the chain of your potential is unveiled.

First is your mental resource strength; the human mind is the fundamental resource; it is the reservoir of all thought and the source of your greatest power—that of choice. Second is your physical resource strength; the body is a servant of the mind; it responds to implanted thoughts and renders results, good or bad. Third is your social resource strength;

it engenders people relationships that mold behavior, character, manners, style, and acceptance. Fourth is your spiritual resource strength, the unseen life force within you; you were created in the image of God; "all things are possible to him that believeth." Mark 9:23.

> There's no defeat in life
> Save from within
> Unless you're beaten there
> You're bound to win.

Build a Resource Gymnasium

Do you practice mind and body conditioning?

The strength, agility, flexibility, and endurance qualities of the mind and body are dependent on thought conditioning. This process is largely determined by one's attitude and values toward life. Nothing can stop a person with the right mental attitude from achieving a goal; nothing can help the person with the wrong mental attitude. Change must come from within.

Maintaining a mental and physical conditioning program is paramount for inroads to progress. The process of conditioning the mind and body creates a cause and effect reaction. The law of growth comes into being. Because of the law of growth the acorn becomes a mighty oak. Because of the law of gravitation the apple falls to the ground. Because of the law of causation, a person becomes as he thinks in his heart. Nothing can happen without its adequate cause.

Mental strength can only be as deep and profound as that which is absorbed through heritage, education, and experience. Today we live in a world of rapid change that has moved from the horse and buggy transport to space travel in just over a half century. Completion of formal education, at any age, immediately begins to lessen in value as technological and social change evolves. The pace of change is increasing on a geometric scale. The adage that "you must run to stay even" is realistic. There are, of course, some things that never change—the beauty of nature's landscape, glory of picturesque stars, smell of the sea. But thought patterns must flow with the ebb and tide of changing environment to grow or even keep abreast.

We have heretofore considered that the body is a servant of the mind. Thus, the body will only respond to our mental direction and this is where the task of conditioning must start. People often aspire to do things which the body is not able to do. The mind is willing but the body is weak. When body fitness is improved a natural thought stimulus occurs to bring body efficiency to a higher level of performance. It is an interesting phenomenon that the balance of these two resources, mind and body, follow. Handicapped people are often able to strengthen one facility to overcome a deficiency in the other.

With a major focus on the nation's declining health during John F. Kennedy's presidency, a national fitness program was launched. Americans everywhere gradually acquired a conscious value of fitness. Towns and cities began to expand recreational facilities. Today masses of runners, joggers, walkers, and others of all ages, are pursuing fitness programs. Medical research renders voluminous reports of proof and support that adequate and controlled exercise contributes to mental and physical well being and longevity. People around the world now recognize the merits of fitness.

I recommend that you build a resource gymnasium—in your mind. This will inspire you to pursue continual mental and physical conditioning for maximum health, longevity, and achievement. Why a gymnasium? It is said that 85 percent of the people search for and thrive on symbols. Gymnasium is a symbol of exercise, conditioning, games, and exhibitions. The word stems from the golden age of Athens and played an important part in the Greek life. Physical strength and grace were highly regarded. A "gymnasion" was a place where athletic exercises were performed. Our word gymnasium has retained that sense of activity, hence becomes a symbol of exercise, conditioning, games, and exhibitions. Apply this symbol to your thought power and use it to develop goals plus an action plan for pursuing continual mind and body conditioning.

The mental gymnasium can be your library at home, community, area academic institutions or wherever courses are offered to help you keep in condition. When learning ceases the mind begins to atrophy. Mental illness, mental apathy, and senility are the grave consequences of inactivity.

Reading is the foundation of wisdom. On this point Leon Gutterman pictures the significance of books: "Without the love of books the richest person is poor, but endowed with this treasure the poorest person is rich. He has wealth which no power can diminish; riches which are always increasing, possessions which the more he scatters the more they accumulate, friends which never desert and pleasures which never die."

Conditioning will follow the action program evolved from thought. It will not happen without deliberate thought. You are the activator. Mental and physical health is just about everything. With it resource power is unlimited. Without it a person carries the burden of growth limitations

Preparation conditions the mind and body to keep pace with progress.

Get Your Act Together

Have you got your act together?
We have discussed the development and use of your mental and physical power resources. Now we shall cover social and spiritual resources then balance all four for maximum achievement potential.

The expression "let's get our act together" is a common one. Coaches often use it to induce their team to pull together, get on the ball, or think seriously about the job at hand. It indicates there is something wrong, out of order, not going according to plan; signals and timing are off; the scheme of things is out of balance. The same comment is heard in the theater, among social groups, and various gatherings. It signifies a need for harmony and balance of power, whether it is in a football game or a chorus line.

A key to competence on any stage whether it be the sports arena, theater, or business meeting is balance and coordination. Those who play sports or perform on stage soon learn that foot work to maintain balance and poise is of utmost importance. It is simply impossible to be competent in a sport or on stage without first mastering these skills. This includes the entire body, that is, arms, legs, feet, and torso; also relative posture and stance. The solution to maximum power exertion is overall balance. It is also the medium for beauty and grace of body action.

Employee performance appraisals often identify an individual as "well-balanced." This implies that appraisers view the employee as one who does have his act together. His human characteristics are pleasing, acceptable, believable, reflect confidence and he is promotable.

I have presented a speech on numerous occasions to varying audiences, young and old, entitled "The Riches of Life." For demonstration purposes I select a chair and label each of the four legs with a word—Mental, Physical, Social, Spiritual. Then I ask the audience, "what would happen if one of the legs was shorter?" Some respond, "the chair would wobble," others, "the chair would be unacceptable—I would look for one with four even legs," or "it would rock, I would find a solid one." An audience picks up the point quickly. Social strength is a balancing leg in life.

Everyone has difficulty in getting along at times. Whether in marriage relationships, manager and subordinate, neighbor or associate, it is important to get along in order to maintain a level of acceptance with your fellow man. Being friendly or a good companion, working in harmony, showing concern for others, being pleasant are all important factors constituting acceptable behavior. Relationships with and acceptance by others serve as the barometer of social strength. To paraphrase Wilfred A. Peterson, noted writer of essays on the *Art of Living,* "Sooner or later a person, if wise, discovers that life is a mixture of good days and bad, victory and defeat, give and take—that people are not any more difficult to get along with in one place than another and that 'getting along' depends about 98 percent on one's own behavior."

When I come to the fourth leg of the chair in the speech, "Riches of Life," which is labeled with the word "spiritual," there is always a quietude that seems to spread over the audience. I invariably sense two messages in the air. One from my Creator who asks, "What will you say to them?" One from the audience who asks, "What will he say that will help me understand—I really do want to be able to sit comfortably on that chair of life." And I say, "I don't know what your beliefs may be, but for me there is magic in believing." "All I have seen teaches me to trust the Creator for all I have not seen," said Emerson. "The man who is diligent in his business will stand before Kings," wrote Solomon centuries ago.

Every person is endowed with some of the divine spirit. It is this incredible unseen life force that seems to render assistance and guidance at just the right time. It is the invisible bond that cements people relationships, strength of character and credibility to stand with confidence. It is the finite power of balance. Have faith. Choose your destiny. Choose wisely. Choose a chair with four legs of equal length. Balance all four of your most precious resources, those of mental, physical, social, and spiritual power, and you shall stand with diligence before kings.

> Doubt sees the obstacles
> Faith sees the way.
> Doubt sees the darkest night
> But faith sees the day.
> Doubt dreads to take a step

But faith soars on high.
Doubt questions—who believes?
Faith answers I!

Preparation opens the power reservoirs of character and soul.

Use Your Creative Imagination

Are you an idea person?

Successful application of resource power is often actuated by a creative imagination. The notion persists that creative ability is some abnormal trait granted only to the gifted. Nothing could be further from the truth. Everyone has some creative ability, much of it latent. It has not been tapped and lies dormant in the mind awaiting discovery.

Many if not all, of your possessions were once only imagined. All the tools and results of technology now proven and in use were once only imagined. The original ideas did not necessarily emanate from the minds of a chosen few. Many came from ordinary people who used their creative powers.

Some great discoveries have resulted from thinking up new problems with no particular goal in mind. The innovators are just curious. Faraday and his curiosity produced electric current. He simply mounted a copper disc between the poles of a horseshoe magnet and spun it.

Polaroid was led by the extraordinarily creative Edwin Land. When a Polaroid research engineer was asked their source of projects he replied, "With Dr. Land around, that is no problem."

Susan Cooper related her experience in doing a student homework assignment that required making a drawing of a flight of stairs. As she finished the drawing and was putting away the ink, a blot dropped right in the middle of the picture. There was insufficient time to draw another. She was upset and in tears. Her father, learning of the trouble said, "Don't worry—all you have to do is draw a dog around it," and she did. The next day the picture was voted best in the class. Often it only needs a little imagination to turn a problem into an advantage.

A group of college students pursuing graduate degrees in management and business was interviewing a young president of a major corporation. When asked how he became president at the age of thirty-nine, he replied, "I asked questions to justify any and every task." The imagination of Senator Robert Kennedy was evident in the use of the statement, "Some people see things as they are and ask why! I see things that never were and ask, why not?" It is the curious mind that explores with excitement to find a better way or solution to a problem; that seeks ways to satisfy or fulfill a potential need. "A person to carry on a successful business must see things in a vision, a dream of the whole thing," said Charles M. Schwab when serving as chairman of Bethlehem Steel.

"Imagination where it is truly creative, is a faculty, not a quality; its seat is in the higher reason, and it is efficient only as a servant of the will. Imagination is mere fantasy— the image making power, common to all who have the gift of dreams," indicated James Russell Lowell.

Einstein considered imagination more powerful than knowledge. When asked the secret of his inventive genius, he replied, "I listen from within." The creative mind has been referred to as a depository of mankind's memories and wisdom by eminent psychologists Jung, Freud, and others. Emmerson called it Infinite Intelligence. The belief and revelation that knowledge of all great minds has existed since the beginning of time opens wide the chasm of potential awareness. You too can unlock the creative power of the higher mind just as the great innovators of the past.

There are several apparent or imagined barriers to thinking creatively. Lack of motivation and curiosity, rushing to irrational conclusions, job restraints, psychological or physiological problems. Many such roadblocks could probably be classed as mental laziness. Many business and social roles are dependent upon innovation. A few imaginative people rise to the surface and take the lead. That role can be yours. Leadership, for example, requires a well-rounded imagination to visualize the cause and solution of day-to-day problems, also to envision potential ones that will most likely occur in the future.

Charles Kettering, General Motors innovative genius and perhaps one of the greatest creative minds of the era said, "All research is simply finding out what is wrong with a thing and then fixing it." This approach is indeed simple and the ideal starting point for the creative thought process. Many researchers and innovators start with a definition of the problem, gather data, put it into rational form then let the subconscious mind concentrate until new ideas come to the surface. These ideas are then worked and reworked, evaluated and tested. When proven, the results enter the endless pipeline of new products or resolved problems. This method is viable for your use too. Visualize it as a sequence of steps.

1. Define the problem in writing. Clarify the requirement and what end result is expected.
2. Gather facts. Obtain all relevant information, talk with other people to gain their awareness and suggestions.
3. Analyze facts. Reduce findings to specific relationships and principles that match the problem definition.
4. Turn to the subconscious. Search for ideas and solutions. Think deeply. Be patient. Don't expect a genie to pop out with an answer immediately.
5. List ideas as they occur. Question the validity of each idea, then search for alternatives and compare. Share your thoughts with others.
6. Select the most logical approach. Put it into design format and test; rework as necessary.

7. Sell your idea. On acceptance or approval fully develop the idea, evaluate, test.

The stars were made for those who look up and whose imagination knows no limitations. Use your creative imagination to supplement the four power resources at your disposal. The learning is in the doing and action is your choice.

Preparation induces creative thought power that fortifies decisions.

Develop a Cooperative Spirit

Are you developing a cooperative spirit with people?

The cliche "it isn't so much what you know as who you know" is often heard in business circles. The truth of this statement is evident in the lives of many who have achieved success in their fields. While knowledge, skills, attitude, and experience are primary tools of great importance in the competitive world, people relationships do set the pace for achievement. Few things can be accomplished on your own. The human role is like a single letter in the alphabet. It can be meaningless, or it can combine with others and be a part of a great meaning.

Seventy large corporations were surveyed to determine what traits they considered most important to employee success. Seventy-five percent ranked the ability to work cooperatively with others at the top of the list. Other dominant factors which surfaced in the survey were ability to communicate effectively, enthusiasm, appearance, balance, and leadership. It is obvious that each of these issues centers on relationships and how people evaluate the factors that concern them.

As you apply the Achievement Quotient formula, $C (P + Q + D) = AQ$, keep in mind that virtually all successful people, past and present, reached their level of accomplishment with the help of others. The formula is not, I repeat, not, designed to use people to secure the material things you love. It emphasizes compassion and devotion for people to help you obtain material things to use. In other words, don't use people and love things; love people and use things.

One of the most involved feats of human cooperation occurred when Neil Armstrong set foot on the moon's surface in July, 1969. Masses of equipment and people were involved over many years to successfully place man on the moon and return to Earth. Continued planetary exploration and launching of the space shuttle orbiter are achievements that depend heavily on harmony of people relationships. These include employees in the plants that manufacture equipment for the astronauts who fly this great array of complex equipment.

"A person is known by the company he keeps"—"Birds of a feather flock together" are relevant aphorisms. I heard a speaker say, "If you want to soar with the eagles you can't sit in a tree and hoot with the owls." If you want to be an achiever, associate with those who are. If your goal is to ultimately hold down a chair of leadership then start developing interests, social and business, that will bring your status up to the level of the role you are seeking. Your written action plan as described in Chapter 3 should include this consideration.

To develop worthy relationships it is important to choose friends and associates who can strongly determine your success. These are people with interests, standards, and values similar to your own; or people who have already reached the role to which you aspire. People associations mirror your character. They reflect the image of characteristics revealed in the aforementioned survey. That is, cooperative spirit, communications ability, enthusiasm, appearance, balance, and leadership qualities. It is just as easy to choose friends and associates who are important, influential and wealthy as it is to choose those whose standards reflect negativism, laziness, or poor attitude toward life.

Social interests are particularly sensitive image areas. If your goal projections involve a role where business entertainment is a factor, then take up golf, tennis or activities compatible with the job. Join clubs that are meaningful to your goals. Do get involved in community programs, with civic clubs, church—accept active roles. People will serve you to the degree you serve them. All such activities build maturity and competence.

Whatever your role is, think of yourself as a salesman. You are constantly on display and marketing your talents and abilities. Observers are either buyers of your services or references for a buyer. Let people know the direction you are headed in life, not by word but through action. Never fail to consider the future significance of what you say or do. Examine your present approach and attitude toward work, personal development, hobbies, social activities, and the tempo of your stride. If the track you are on leads nowhere, look at yourself. Maybe it's time to switch tracks and get on one that leads toward your goals.

An old Persian proverb is a fitting reference:

> He who knows not,
>   And knows not that he knows not,
>   Is a fool—shun him.
>
> He who knows not,
>   And knows that he knows not
>   Is a child—teach him,
>
> He who knows,
>   And knows not that he knows,
>   Is asleep—wake him.
>
> He who knows,
>   And knows that he knows
>   Is wise—follow him.

Preparation reveals personal standards and the cooperative spirit of people.

93

Adopt Attitude of Tolerance

Do you practice self-restraint?

For want of self-restraint many people spend their lives struggling with problems and difficulties of their own making. Their stage of life is in constant turmoil as a result of intolerance, while others who may be much less talented set a harmonious environment and achieve success by self-restraint.

The annals of history unfold six words of admonition that will provoke harmony in human relationships;

Control Thyself—Cicero
Know Thyself—Socrates
Give Thyself—Christ

John Locke emphasized the strength of tolerance in words worthy of etching on the mind: "The most precious of all our possessions is power over ourselves; power to withstand trial, to bear suffering, to confront dangers; power over pleasure and pain; power to follow our convictions, however resisted by menace and scorn; the power of calm reliance in scenes of darkness and storms."

Anything worth having involves a price represented by work, self-sacrifice, love and tolerance. These are positive virtues. Intolerance leads to anger, in turn, to adverse consequences. Proverbs 16:32 states "he that is slow to anger is better than the mighty; and he that ruleth his spirit than he that taketh a city."

Few things will rise to the surface faster than feelings. For example we are quick to respond to a loud voice by raising our own. Inability to control emotions of anger is a distinct handicap in human relations and must be dealt with throughout our lives. Because of this fact it is often difficult to restrain and control ourselves at the right time. We lose sight of the value of being a good listener.

Leaders in business and other activities are often guilty of using the power of their voices and titles when projects are not on time, goals not achieved, production levels are down, or deliveries not made. Indeed most people raise havoc about similar issues with local merchants and just about any other source. It always seems easier to blow off steam, lay blame than to seek reason or solutions. The true power of our resources is replaced, with limited results, by emotional response and blood pressure.

Human emotions know no laws of logic. But common sense tells us there is no mileage to be gained through passion, temper or tantrums. If you have ever stirred up a hornet's nest and suffered the wrath of bee stings then you have experienced the effects of temper and madness. Only pain resulted.

For meaningful human relationships visualize that tolerance builds harmony as in song; intolerance brews wrath and pain like the sting of a hornet. Listening will resolve more problems than shouting. Seek problem solutions rather than guilty contributors. Build values in human relationships by example. Your success depends on it.

Preparation with an attitude of tolerance eliminates stress and worry.

And now a recapitulation of the ideas presented in this chapter plus the apothegms:

1. You are heir to a kingdom. All things are possible to him that believeth. Organize and utilize your God-given resources.
2. Build a resource gymnasium and practice mental and physical conditioning on a regular schedule.
3. For greatest returns get your act together by balancing all resources like four legs of equal length on a chair.
4. Creative imagination is a faculty common to all. Use it wisely to solve today's problems or for discovery of things yet unknown.
5. Choose friends and associates compatible with your goals, and interests; those who can influence your success. A caution— don't use people and love things, but love people and use things.

6. The power of self-control is within you. It is a precious possession with which to build your life's ladder of achievement.

APOTHEGMS

1. *Preparation conditions the mind and body to keep pace with progress.*
2. *Preparation opens the power reservoirs of character and soul.*
3. *Preparation induces creative thought power that fortifies decisions.*
4. *Preparation reveals personal standards and the cooperative spirit of people.*
5. *Preparation with an attitude of tolerance eliminates stress and worry.*

7

Communication Power

A word fitly spoken is like apples of gold in pictures of silver.
—Proverbs 25:11

(PREPARATION)

Are you an effective speaker?

Few talents will propel a person faster or farther than the ability to speak effectively. Speech reveals man's thoughts, depth of knowledge, experience and awareness. Thoughts are the source of all ideas, good or ill. "As a vessel is known by the sound whether it be cracked or not, so men are proved by their speeches whether they be wise or foolish," spoke Demosthenes. Some of history's great leaders were perhaps noted first for their speech and second for their leadership. The ability to speak effectively propelled to the top such leaders as Abraham Lincoln, Franklin Roosevelt, Winston Churchill, John Kennedy, Martin Luther King, and many others. Their speech was forceful, dynamic, explicit, harmonious, and moving. They influenced millions through words and the power of the tongue.

Today, industry and business leaders who rise to top roles

must be more effective communicators than in former years. Priorities have changed due to extensive media coverage. The miracle of instant worldwide news coverage via satellite, coupled with government regulatory intervention, brings media and business leaders in constant contact. Hence, the young executive aspiring to move up the ladder must be conscious of the need to be an effective communicator. Those who are not learning to speak effectively will find their career leveling off at a lower plateau than desired due to the lack of polish in this vital skill.

Many companies have structured special in-house communications training programs for their employees. Many encourage personnel to pursue training through community programs and seminars. Toastmasters International, Santa Ana, California, the world's largest organization devoted to communications and leadership development, has had spectacular growth since its beginning in 1924.

This organization is devoted to the basic principles of effective speech, its application in making presentations and leading meetings. Good speaking habits are a result of mastering principles, techniques and polishing them through practice and evaluation. Three primary steps are required to achieve excellence. They are practice, practice, practice.

Speak Your Way to Success

Are you confident in speaking to groups?

It is my desire to help you become a more successful speaker. Therefore, I would like to eliminate the one common obstacle for many—fear. If fear is preventing you from taking that first step in developing your speaking skills, relax. It is a natural emotion. You can overcome it in a brief period. In my communication seminars I have experienced some students who could not get out of their chair. A fear impulse seemed to freeze them to the seat. Some have even felt nauseous. After brief counseling, most will take the first step with trepidation, the second with caution, the third with self-assurance. After that there is no holding back for those who really want to grow.

Nervousness and anxiety are natural reactions. Even the experienced speakers and others who go on stage have momentary feelings about the reaction of an audience. But the knowledge of their material and confidence gained through experience overcomes quickly. An audience will know immediately if a speaker is fearful or confident.

Two important and vital steps are suggested to overcome fear; they are relaxation and visualization. Thereafter, take a third step and speak before an audience for practice. First relax. Some people do have difficulty simply because they do not know how to relax. They experience tenseness about many things. This, of course, is unhealthy. You can learn and practice simple relaxation techniques. Do this: take a comfortable position, seated or lying down, close your eyes. Tense and relax the muscles of the body starting with the toes, moving up the leg and thigh muscles, stomach, back, arms, fingers, jaws, and forehead. Now affirm calming thoughts to yourself. Breathe deeply. Practice this routine for about ten minutes daily and learn to relax. Do seek professional advice if this seems appropriate.

The next step is visualization. Create and visualize mental images of audience situations in meeting rooms or auditoriums. Practice this technique until you sense familiarity with the picture. Too, as you observe and listen to speakers at meetings, church, or elsewhere, close your eyes and imagine yourself in the speaker's position. You will doubtless discover the words being spoken are not new. But the speaker probably is confident and has the ability to get the message across.

Take the next step and practice before an audience. If opportunities are not available in your work environment, then seek outside audiences. One of the best audiences for the beginner would be a Toastmasters Club. The club structure is designed for people to learn and practice the art of speaking. Highly developed educational materials at nominal cost provide the guidelines. Experienced members serve as evaluators to help others develop their talents. The learning is in the doing. Therefore, search for appropriate speech training programs and seminars. Get involved and practice. You can speak your way to success. Many have and most probably commenced with no more to offer than the desire to achieve.

Preparation spawns eloquence of self-expression and reveals self-confidence.

Know What Audiences Expect

Can you satisfy an audience with words?

Have you ever listened to speakers who did not relate to the audience, were poorly prepared, and their delivery put many to sleep? Many such presentations are made daily to bored audiences. It evidences a lack of speech training, inadequate preparation and little concern for the interests of an audience.

The primary requirement in any speech is that the contents relate to the needs of an audience. This is where many presenters miss the mark and are classed as boring. Speakers who do not relate to others' needs are just talking to themselves. It is important to always obtain the general facts about an audience in advance so that your words will definitely focus on their interests.

Successful speeches generally depend on four factors: how you look (appearance); what you say (message); how you say it (delivery); what you do (mannerisms). As reported by Richard Allen Stull, President of Speakers Bureau International, Las Vegas, Nevada, a survey conducted by his firm covering 600 associations and 120 corporations, and representing over 5,000 meetings, indicated the following audience expectations and evaluation of speakers: Nonprofessional speakers were judged 20 percent on appearance, 70 percent on message, 8 percent on enthusiasm, and 2 percent on humor. The professional speaker was judged roughly

50 percent on appearance, 20 percent on content, 1b percent on enthusiasm, and 15 percent on humor. The survey listed 60 percent of the speakers as associations, corporate executives and specialists, 20 percent politicians, 15 percent professional speakers, and 5 percent celebrities. Audiences expect more message from the nonprofessional and more entertainment from the professional.

While evaluations and expectations vary widely, it is apparent that audiences focus on the four factors of appearance, message, delivery, and mannerisms.

Speeches may be classified in three categories: (1) to inform, (2) to persuade, and (3) amuse or entertain. The first presents few problems since it is merely passing information to others such as announcements, policy changes, work assignments, and similar issues. The second is the most common among general audiences, and certainly in the business world. The third, to entertain, utilizes jokes, stories, one-liners, and anecdotes. The speaker is called a humorist. An effective humorist combines a natural sense of wit and sensitivity to the enjoyment of laughter. Regardless of the category of speech being presented, informing, persuading or entertaining, the message must relate to audience interests for acceptance.

Preparation to satisfy the needs of people insures progress.

Build Presentations in Logical Steps

Do your messages flow with logic?
An effective speech should be as melodious as a song. The tune should flow in harmony with embellishments and modulations. It should contain a memorable message, a tune that you want others to hum or sing.

Speeches should comprise an attention-getting opener that encompasses a premise, a body containing three to five points—preferably no more than three, and a close that summarizes the body or restates the premise. The structure of your speech should be similar to the structure and erection of a building. For example, a speech and a building must start with a purpose; an entrance represents the opening; framework and contents are the body, and exit is the close.

As you prepare your speech, recognize that getting the presentation off to the right start is a key to audience acceptance. Don't apologize. A speaker's warmth is the first thing felt by an audience whether it be one of five thousand people, and whether it be a business meeting or a convention. Warmth is best represented by a smile, the biggest you can generate. This should be followed by words of compliment to the arrangers and welcome to the audience. Everyone must feel good about being there to hear your comments. Warming up routines are usually followed by the professional to put an audience at ease or get them in a receptive mood. Similar ice-breaking comments are appropriate in business meetings. Any message will be better received by a receptive audience. Introductory routines such as opening stories for warm up serve this purpose. Opening statements to the meat of the speech should be attention getting, create curiosity, appeal to audience interest. A startling question or challenging statement are considered the strongest openers.

I recommend developing a general outline for the framework and contents rather than attempting to write out the speech initially. Using 3″ x 5″ cards, I jot down thoughts as they come to mind, later sort into logical sequence, then write out the planned presentation. To keep the speech on track, I put it together in units. For example, if I planned to make one point in a short speech, I give a statement of the premise, support by an example or anecdote to prove the point, and call for action or audience agreement on the premise. For a longer speech I use three to five points following a six-step sequence and expand or contract to match the allotted time. The six-step sequence is:

1. Premise or problem.
2. Support with statement of reason or by quote from ancient or current authority.

3. Expand with an example or quote a poetic or biblical source to magnify.
4. Tell an anecdote to support.
5. Tell a story about myself or ordinary person to magnify.
6. Restate premise—call for action or agreement.

The unit concept is easy to develop, lends itself to simple memory techniques and offers an audience picturesque speech for maximum retention.

Closings should summarize or restate premise, the problem or solution. These can be embellished with verse or humor. Many professionals prefer to close on a high note, frequently with a story that sends the audience off with a good feeling. When a presentation starts on a high note, flows with good modulation of timely examples, humor, stories, and closes on a high note, audience interest is sustained. It becomes an enjoyable experience for both the speaker and the listener.

Following a logical sequence of steps from the opening through the body outline, and close in developing your next presentation can make it memorable for the listeners.

Preparation of speech organizes thoughts in harmonious logic.

Master Effective Characteristics

Do you present a winning platform style?
Two factors constitute the quality of an effective speaker. They are style and message. We have discussed the value of a well-prepared message. Style is represented by a number of factors, including:

Delivery	Pronunciation	Voice
Mannerisms	Enunciation	Eye Contact
Body Language	Grammar	Appearance

DELIVERY STYLE should be your own. The best style is a natural one. While you may have the ability to mimic some outstanding personality, it is quite possible that your delivery style when developed will lead to greater heights. Thus, unless you intend to be an impersonator or mimic, stick with your own style and build on it.

MANNERISMS and GESTURES constitute expression, affectations, movements, use of body and feet, hands and arms, head and face to add meaning and feeling to your presentation. Controlled, meaningful gestures give picturesque, silent expression to speech.

Posture, stance, and emotion form a direct link. The wandering, walking speaker usually keeps the audience attention on wandering and walking. The emotional hand talker generates the same problem. Good erect balanced posture with casual movements reflects strength and commands attention. When the head is held high, eyes on the audience, face reflecting a slight smile, self-confidence exudes. Conversely, when a speaker stands with slouched shoulders, head drooping, an image of depression and lack of confidence comes through.

Use meaningful hand and facial gestures to give expression to your words. Gestures should reflect pictures that add color, dynamism, and character.

BODY LANGUAGE, often called KINESICS, is the oldest form of communication and often more accurate than words. Speaking words that are untrue or exaggerated is easier than pretending to be sincere or friendly through kinesics. Listeners will not accept your word with confidence if the expression through the ears is different than the one seen through the eyes.

It must be stated that no body position such as folded arms, crossed legs or movement connotes a precise meaning. Scientists have endeavored to determine consistency of meaning in body actions, but have found the same actions may mean various things. For example, drumming fingers on a table may mean stress or the person may be imagining the beat of music. An erect confident looking person walking at a fast pace may indicate only the awareness of where he is going; it could be an important meeting or the bathroom.

Body communications and the spoken word or thought patterns are dependent upon each other. Body language should not be taken too seriously. However, it is very important to be conscious of this form of nonverbal communication. Acceptance or rejection of your ideas, leadership strength, or requests depends on the visible behavior and emotions exhibited by you and your listeners. Polish your nonverbal skills for use in speech. Be observant of body communications among your listeners. When a listener falls asleep you know he is bored. If he falls off the chair, take credit for awakening him.

PRONUNCIATION and ENUNCIATION casts an image of your knowledge, education, experience, culture, and probably the locale of your birth. Every time you speak your mind is on parade.

> Speak clearly, if you speak at all
> Carve every word before you let it fall.

Common weaknesses in pronunciation and enunciation center on carelessness, airs, and exactness. Most audiences are conscious of accepted standards in educated speech and this may vary from one locale to another. However, substituting a "d" for the "th" as in dese, dat, and dose reflects slovenly speech. Dropping the "g" in words ending in "ing" as in "fishin'," "workin'," "walkin' " is another form of poor speech.

Uncommon pronunciations of the words either as "eyether," neither as "neyether" generate emotional response by the listener and take his mind off the message. Exactness of word pronunciation, that is, slowly and deliberately highlighting syllables tends to obscure thought patterns and influences receptivity. One must be conscious of good word usage to be an effective speaker, but when carried to extremes, it will detract from the intended power of speech.

If this is a problem for you, read appropriate books on improving your vocabulary or take courses that will overcome the weakness.

GRAMMAR represents the words in which you dress your ideas. Don't dress your ideas in patched clothes. Carelessness in using tenses of verbs and nouns, complicated lengthy sentence formations, and off-color, inappropriate slang are a reflection of poor grammar and choice of words. Word fillers such as "ah," "anda," "you know," detract from the quality of speech. Most audiences readily accept reasonable attention to good grammar. Simple sentences simply spoken are preferred. Adapt language to the audience. Talk in people terms. Use language that fits your personality—Will Rogers did it with great success. Use phrases that create pictures. There is no substitute for proper word usage. Polish your grammar, drop the word fillers, and display your talents through word power.

VOICE quality supports or undermines the importance of your words. Voice characteristics that please are: friendly tones; normal pitch so it does not crack on emphatic words; every sentence completed in audible tone; tempo slow enough for understanding, fast enough to insure listener interest; loud and clear enough to reach the last row of the audience. Voices that displease are: harsh, belligerent in tone; pitch too high; scolding delivery; final words of sentence suppressed as though swallowed; emphasis placed on unimportant words.

Voice control is influenced by proper breathing; exhaling or gulping breaths affect pitch and pace of speech. Seek to project your voice without shouting; speak in pleasant tones at a reasonable pace for clarity and understanding.

EYE CONTACT with people creates a personal feeling of confidence and rapport with the speaker. Therefore speak to people, not to the floor, ceiling, walls, or lectern. Hold eye contact momentarily on one person as thoughts unfold. Then move slowly from person to person covering the entire audience when practical. Don't scan an audience. This creates the impression that you are talking to yourself. Speaking into the eyes of many people in an audience follows the same routine as speaking one on one except you deliberately move from person to person.

APPEARANCE should suit the occasion. I recommend that you follow the formula, "Occasion and environment equal attire." To sell a speech you must sell yourself. Thus, appearance is a significant factor. People do not enjoy buying from one who does not look the role being played. Mutual trust is absent. Choose attire wisely for any speaking opportunity. Look your best for the best performance. You are a salesperson. Sell yourself and your abilities.

Preparation and polish of a speaking style is a step toward professionalism.

Use Humor Wisely

Do people laugh at your humor?

Most people enjoy humor and most speakers want to generate laughter. Of all the devices for getting and holding the attention of an audience, humor has proven the most effective. Timely humor does add color and enjoyment to speech when used to magnify points and when told in good style. There are very few occasions when humor is inappropriate. Thus, learning to use it will add quality, variety and audience acceptance of your presentation.

Humor is anything which causes an audience to laugh. Max Eastman, in his book *Enjoyment of Laughter* (copyright 1936, by Max Eastman, published by Simon and Schuster, Inc.), offers four laws in explaining the science of humor. These provide an excellent base for understanding and using humor.

The first law of humor is that things can be funny only when we are in fun. We may be only "half in fun" and still funny. But when we are not in fun at all, when we are in dead earnest, humor is the thing that is dead.

The second law is that when we are in fun, a peculiar shift of values takes place. Pleasant things are still pleasant, but disagreeable things so long as they are not disagreeable enough to "spoil the fun" tend to acquire a pleasant emotional flavor and provoke a laugh.

The third law is that "being in fun" is a condition most natural to childhood, and that children at play reveal the humorous laugh in its simplest form. To them every unmanageable, ugly, disgusting, deceiving, jolting, banging, or disturbing thing, unless it be calamitous enough to force them out of the mood of play, is enjoyable and funny.

The fourth law is that grown-up people retain in varying degrees this aptitude for being in fun, and thus enjoying unpleasant things as funny. But those not richly endowed with humor manage to feel a very comic feeling only when within, behind, beyond, or suggested by, the playful unpleasant thing, there is a pleasant one. Only then do they laugh uproariously like playing children.

Humor comes in many forms. The funny story, one-liners, exaggeration, and daffynition are a few. But why use humor? Every speaker knows that he must develop techniques for getting and holding attention. Equally important is to use every known method of getting people to listen, and sometimes that is very difficult. A teacher yelled at one of her students saying, "Pay a little attention." The student replied, "I'm paying as little attention as I can." Television has influenced our visual world and the desire for entertainment. Therefore, speeches must be developed and delivered to match the mode of today's audience interests.

Humor will earn a beneficial reputation for the speaker; audiences will tell others of a speaker's good or bad qualities. Humor creates good feelings and will generate good will. A speaker can be more persuasive when humor is used. When people are in a pleasant mood, they are more receptive.

A few don't's are offered as guidelines. When in doubt don't use humor. Don't tell stories for the sake of telling stories—each story must be related to the occasion or objective of the speech. Don't use humor if the occasion does not call for it, such as areas when tension or grief is present.

Don't tell stories unless you have practiced and practiced them so you can tell them in your words. Make yourself the brunt of stories often. Don't make people in the audience the brunt of a joke unless you have discussed it with the person or persons involved and know it will be accepted in fun. Don't tell off-color stories—the risk of offending is great.

Do use humor when it suits the occasion. Intersperse humor throughout a speech, say every three to five minutes, to keep an audience stimulated. Keep stories relevant; make sure a story relates to the idea being developed.

Each person must develop his own style of delivery. While some laugh at their own humor, the object is to entertain the audience. Use the approach that best suits your makeup and generates the most favorable response.

Timing is the key to use of humor and this takes practice. Before making a presentation, first practice your humor over and over to clearly establish the thread of the story and the punch line firmly in your mind. Practice before a mirror to observe facial expressions and gestures. Try out your humor on a trusting critic before trying on a large audience.

For a greater insight into humor and its use, consider the array of books available on the subject in your library or bookstore.

It is said that man was given an imagination to compensate him for what he is not—and a sense of humor was provided him to console him for what he is. Develop your sense of humor for best results in speech.

Preparation and timely use of humor enhances message value.

Magnify with Visual Aids

Do you supplement your speech with aids?
A visual aid can communicate an idea more quickly, clearly, and vividly than any other means of communication.

Visuals lend variety and interest to speech. They serve to illuminate words. The old Chinese proverb, "One picture is worth a thousand words," is never disputed. You increase communications with an audience by a new dimension—sight.

There are speakers who can make their subjects very clear through words and word pictures. But for most, a diagram or picture makes a point faster and better. Ideas are accepted with greater ease and understanding. Too, viewers' retention time is increased.

Visuals include a variety of devices such as transparencies, slides, films, video, charts, posters, flannel boards, mockups, cutaway models, and displays. Don't complicate a presentation with complex visuals. Simplicity is divine. Select and use those that will help make or magnify a point. It is advisable to always select or use visuals of good quality. Poor quality will detract from the presentation whereas good quality enhances.

Commercial sources offer many off-the-shelf items that give a professional and artistic touch. However, ordinary chart paper and colored water pens or pencils are worthy and less expensive alternatives. Therefore, first consider the aids that will fill your needs and enhance your presentation.

The size of the audience generally determines the choice and size of aids to be used. Everyone in viewing and hearing range must be able to see and hear or they will feel left out. Words and diagrams must be of appropriate size for all viewers to see and read. Avoid too much detail on the visual.

Speaker location relative to visuals is important. Always stand in a position where you can easily and comfortably guide the eyes of the viewing audience to specific details on the visual with your hand or a pointer. The viewers' eyes will invariably follow your hand or the pointer as you identify key words, points, or picture details. If you fail to direct the viewers' eyes they will automatically try to read or interpret an entire visual; they will not hear your words of explanation.

When discussing a chart or picture, don't block the view; make sure all can see. And don't talk to the visual. Face and talk to the audience. Here are some tips on the use of exhibits, flip charts, and graphs:

1. Use for small groups.
2. Use large letters/pictures.
3. Use to illustrate/magnify.
4. Treat a single idea on each visual. Keep it simple.
5. Use colors to add sparkle and contrast.
6. Reveal only to make a point, then cover or put aside.

For overhead, strip and slide projectors:

1. Use for small or large audiences.
2. Use to portray accuracy of design, or statistics.
3. Keep detail to a minimum.
4. Use only to make a point, then cover or put aside.

Video is also a popular aid. Industry and business have found many uses to supplement training and educational programs. Standard video projection limits the number of viewers per video, however, larger viewing screens are available and may be worthy of consideration.

Handle all visuals with tender care. They are your aids. Careful handling conveys a silent message of their value to the viewer. I repeat, use visuals only as an aid, never as a crutch. Uncover or disclose only when you are ready to use them, then cover or remove from sight when the purpose has been served. If they remain exposed naturally viewers will keep focusing on the visual and not listen to what you are saying. Remember too, don't talk to visuals; face and talk to the audience.

Preparation and use of visual aids clarifies communications.

Evaluate Your Progress

Are you aware of your weaknesses in speech?

Observers and listeners are constantly forming opinions each time you communicate—at home, on the job, or in social gatherings. Personal growth and progress through speech and other forms of communication are a measure of what others think. While it is important to feel good about one's self, reinforcement, praise and constructive criticism from concerned evaluators is essential for growth.

Your effectiveness as a speaker, writer, or listener depends on the degree to which you study, practice and polish these skills. Orsion S. Marden said, "The ability to communicate well is to a man what cutting and polishing are to a rough diamond. The grinding does not add anything. It merely reveals its wealth." In order to apply polish where it will do the most good, it is invaluable to seek evaluation from select critics or from an entire audience. I know one professional speaker who passes evaluation cards throughout each audience asking for evaluation of his presentation. Not everyone is that courageous. But it has paid off for this speaker; he constantly adds polish and is today a very popular speaker in great demand. The evaluation should logically focus on the four steps outlined in the section of this chapter, "Know What Audiences Expect." These are: how you look, what you say, how you say it, and what you do. Evaluations need not be complex but should relate to the major qualities of speech—style and message.

I recommend selecting one or more astute and helpful people to evaluate each of your presentations with emphasis on: The message—its structure, opening, points, examples, humor, close. The characteristics—mannerisms, voice, eye contact, pronunciation, enunciation, grammar, appearance. The mechanics—use of the lectern or stage, notes, microphone, timing. For simplicity, ask evaluators to give you a "three-C sandwich" appraisal: Compliment the things done well. Criticize the things done poorly. Constructively suggest how to improve weaknesses.

112

Everyone in an audience is an evaluator. To achieve satisfactory progress as a communicator it behooves us to be aware of what others think. Keep an open mind and evaluation will help raise your achievement quotient.

Preparation with awareness of weaknesses stimulates the desire to reach for greatness.

Get Results in Group Meetings

Are your meetings productive?

Most people attend or run meetings in business or community functions. While some meetings are well organized and productive, many are considered a waste of time and a costly way of doing business. Meetings are discussed herein primarily from the viewpoint of the leader.

The wide variety of meetings held preclude offering rules per se that suggest there is only one way to conduct a productive meeting. But there are general guidelines and principles that will help. My purpose is to offer useful tools for your reference.

As a leader, start your consideration of a meeting by asking, "Is a meeting necessary?" Make sure that a meeting is the only way to accomplish your objectives before proceeding.

There are five general classifications of meetings. These are: Information—Giving; Information—Getting; Information—Exchanging; Problem Solving; Instructional/Educational. I am excluding those meetings which follow specific rituals.

Meeting preparation must start with a purpose or objective. When this is clearly defined then the agenda, selection of participants and meeting arrangements can be pursued. Once again I recommend the use of the adage by Rudyard Kipling to plan your meeting—"I have six honest serving men, they taught me all I know; Their names are Why—What—Who—How—Where—When." By applying these six factors all key issues for a useful meeting are covered, thus:

- Purpose or Objective   (Why)
- Agenda   (What)
- Participants   (Who)
- Arrangements   (How)
- Place   (Where)
- Time   (When)

Conducting a successful meeting depends on the personality of the leader and knowledge of the participants. Following is a list of steps that will generally serve to guide the most frequently held meetings—information and problem solving:

1. OPEN meetings on time and stick to the time schedule listed on the agenda.
2. WELCOME participants; they should feel good about attending. Establish a friendly atmosphere. State length of meeting and stick to schedule.
3. PURPOSE or OBJECTIVES must be stated and made clear at the outset so everyone attending can concentrate on the issues to be covered. This eliminates hidden agendas and keeps participants on track. Then define meeting procedures, discussion routines and set ground rules as necessary.
4. PREASSIGNMENTS should be made when prepared data is required to support or supplement discussion.
5. DISCUSSION must be guided by the leader to keep participants on the objectives or subject. Keep discussion free of personalities. Each participant should have an opportunity to contribute.
6. QUESTIONS and ANSWERS are worthy as a means of creating understanding and good feelings. When questions arise, repeat them to the group as necessary to insure clarity, then respond to the audience, not to the questioner. When appropriate refer questions to the group for discussion.
7. SUMMARIZE the meeting for all participants and crystallize group thinking. This creates a clear understand-

ing of discussion and describes action steps that are to follow.

8. THANK participants for attending and sharing time.
9. CLOSE meeting on time.

At the conclusion evaluate your leadership and the meeting results by asking yourself three important questions:

1. Did the meeting fill a need?
2. Were objectives accomplished on time?
3. Were participants satisfied?

To eliminate personal bias verify your evaluation by discussing with some of the participants. Meetings can be run effectively and your achievement quotient will rise through good leadership.

Preparation based on sound principles is a step toward excellence.

A review of the highlights in each chapter section and the apothegms will be helpful as you seek growth through speech and conducting productive meetings.

1. Business leaders who rise to the top in today's competitive, media-oriented environment must be more effective communicators than in former years.
2. Eliminate fear, nervousness, and anxiety through relaxation and visualization, then pursue the development of speaking skills. Three key requisites are: practice—practice—practice.
3. Four factors serve as guidelines for successful communicators: These are how you look (appearance); what you say (message); how you say it (delivery); what you do (mannerisms).
4. Logical flow of a message, segregated into specific points, supported by adequate examples, embellished with humor when appropriate contributes to understanding and acceptance.
5. Style is represented by characteristics of delivery, mannerisms, and appearance. Use a natural style—your own. Body language and meaningful gestures add sparkle and interest. Appearance is a reflection of your values.

6. Timely humor creates good feelings in others when used in good taste. Keep stories relevant; humor must relate to the idea being developed to be effective.
7. Visual aids are more effective than any other means of communication. They illuminate words. Use to enhance speech and create understanding.
8. Apply evaluation techniques for maximum growth. It is important to see your weaknesses as others see them. This not only highlights areas for development, but also keeps you humble.
9. Organize and run productive meetings by using Kipling's six honest serving men, "WHY—WHAT—WHO—HOW—WHERE—WHEN." Keep on time and on track with well-planned agendas.

APOTHEGMS

1. *Preparation spawns eloquence of self-expression and reveals self-confidence.*
2. *Preparation to satisfy the needs of people insures progress.*
3. *Preparation of speech organizes thoughts in harmonious logic.*
4. *Preparation and polish of a speaking style is a step toward professionalism.*
5. *Preparation and timely use of humor enhances message value.*
6. *Preparation and use of visual aids clarifies communications.*
7. *Preparation with awareness of weaknesses stimulates the desire to reach for greatness.*
8. *Preparation based on sound principles in a step toward excellence.*

8
Competence Power

Wood burns because it has the proper stuff in it; and a man becomes famous because he has the proper stuff in him.

—Johann Wolfgang von Goethe

(QUALITY)

The voyage to various ports of call now takes you to the harbor of QUALITY for an all-important visit through ten imagery sources for building competence power. Quality is the second of three factors in the Achievement Quotient formula multiplier, $C (P + Q + D) = AQ$.

Are you fully competent to reach your goals?

Few will admit that they are as competent as they could be or expect to be in time. Each day offers another degree of knowledge and experience on which to further mold total competency and, in turn, shape destiny.

Competence power may be compared to a light bulb. The light bulb is dependent on the strength of its elements which establish the wattage and output. Man's output power is also dependent on the strength of the elements that comprise his total ability. This power represents the ability to perform within the top limits of one's preparedness. It is

117

doing the best that you know how to do. Anything less is simply energy gone to waste.

Some years ago a carpenter went to a blacksmith and asked him to make a hammer as good as he knew how. The carpenter explained that he and several other carpenters had come to town to work on a new church and he had forgotten his hammer. The blacksmith said, "Perhaps you would not want to pay for a hammer as good as I know how to make." "Yes, I do," said the carpenter. "I want a good hammer."

The hammer turned out the best the carpenter had ever seen, probably the best ever made. The blacksmith had shaped the head so that the handle would not slip out and the head would not fly off. The carpenter boasted to his companions of the quality of the hammer. It was truly the best any of them had seen. The next day the other carpenters went to the blacksmith and each ordered the same type hammer. When the contractor saw the tools, he ordered two for himself, asking that they be made a little better than those for the carpenters. "I can't make any better ones," said the blacksmith. "When I make a thing, I make it as well as I can, no matter who it is for." Word spread about the craftsman's quality product. The blacksmith continued to make only one type of hammer for many years. The best that he could possibly make.

The growth opportunities that blossom for the one who is able, qualified, and ready to make a better widget and fill a need are more plentiful today than any time in history. On this point Emerson speaks with usual candor: "If a man can write a better book, preach a better sermon, or make a better mousetrap than his neighbor, though he build his house in the woods, the world will make a beaten path to his door." In the poetic lines of Douglas Malloch "Be The Best At Whatever You Are":

> If you can't be a pine on the top of a hill
> Be a shrub in the valley but be

The best little shrub by the side of the hill.
Be a bush if you can't be a tree.

If you can't be a bush be a bit of grass
And some highway happier make;
If you can't be a muskie then just be a bass
But be the liveliest bass in the lake.

We can't all be captains, we've got to be crew,
There is something for all of us. There
Is big work to do and there's lesser to do
And the task we must do is the near.

If you can't be a highway then just be a trail;
If you can't be the sun be a star;
It isn't by size that you win or you fail.
Be the best of whatever you are.

In the chapter sections that follow I shall lead you through the major elements that build competence power. As in nearly all human effort the output and its application by the end user, other people, will render judgment as to quality and service. This, in turn, identifies the competency level of the producer. Make a better hammer, build a better mousetrap. Find a need and fill it. The world awaits you—the discoverer and builder.

Build on Your Qualifications

Are you preparing to meet tomorrow's challenges?

Fortune favors the one who is prepared. "Before anything else, getting ready is the secret of success," said Henry Ford. Luck is the meeting point of preparation and opportunity; obstacles are merely unrecognized opportunities.

I am a great believer in luck, and I find the harder I work and prepare for the road ahead, the more luck I have.

The Chinese write the word crisis in two characters, one of which means "danger" and the other "opportunity." Competence for the tasks at hand and the ones ahead implies preparedness; possessing knowledge and skill to accept the challenges and opportunities that come your way. One does not wait for a job opening and then say, "it's time to prepare." Preparation is a constant and smooth pace toward fulfillment of goals and action plans. Preparation implies that you are making deposits to your mental bank account in readiness for opportunity.

In Italy, a man fell heir to a small typewriter factory that was just making ends meet. In twenty years he transformed the business into the largest maker of office equipment in Europe and captured a worldwide market. He attributed the business success to a simple formula, "To know; to make; to make known." His name was Olivetti.

Competence is to know; it allows one to convert knowledge, skills, and experience into something tangible and to become known for overall qualifications. More than 80 percent of these qualifications will be in the development of personal attributes such as initiative, thoroughness, concentration, decision, adaptability, and leadership. Personal growth is largely dependent on the degree to which these characteristics are cultivated in readiness for the next opportunity.

Study your personal goals and action plans. They represent the pathway for building your qualifications. If your goals and plans have not been formed in sound thought you may be erecting a one-story edifice with no exit. Build a multi-story structure that leads to greater heights. Oliver Wendell Holmes classified achievers like buildings with skylights: "There are one-story intellects, two-story intellects, and three-story intellects with skylights. All fact collectors, who have no aim beyond their facts, are one-story men. Two-story men compare, reason, generalize, using the labors of the fact collectors as well as their own. Three-story men idealize, imagine, predict; their best illumination comes from above, through the skylight."

The eagle was once nothing but an egg, but what would we know about the nature, the meaning, the possibilities of that egg had we never seen the eagle soaring against the sky. You, too, are a miracle of life. There are no limits on the opportunities before you. Each one calls for specific qualifications. Determine in advance the qualifications required to satisfy your aim. Then let competence serve as your benchmark.

Quality is founded in the desire and commitment to excel.

Assume Responsibility for Actions

Do you have the courage to shoulder responsibility?

There is a price tag on personal growth. That price is the willingness to assume the responsibility of an assigned office, position, or role and the actions taken. Business is dependent upon action. It cannot go forward by indecision, complacency, vacillation, passing the buck. Those in positions of leadership must support their actions with facts and be responsible for the decisions made. The willingness to accept and handle responsibility with common sense is a prerequisite to progress and leadership positions.

A ladder of achievement portraying willingness to reach for rungs of responsibility and the probable response are viewed in relative ratios, thus:

100%—I did
90%—I will
80%—I can
70%—I think I can
60%—I might
50%—I think I might
40%—What is it?
30%—I wish I could
20%—I don't know how
10%—I can't
0%—I won't

121

Peter Drucker, noted author and professor of management, wrote in his book *Management—Tasks—Responsibilities—Practices* (Copyright 1973, 1974, published by Harper & Row), "Our society has become, within an incredible short fifty years, a society of institutions. To make our institutions perform responsibly, autonomously, and on a high level of achievement is thus the only safeguard of freedom and dignity in the pluralist society of institutions. It is the performance of the management and managers of our institutions—business and government, society and culture—which will determine our present and future." He comments further, "Management is a practice rather than a science. Its practice is based both on knowledge and on responsibility." It should be apparent that to rise to the top you must be willing and able to shoulder responsibility—to say "I can," "I will," "I did."

In recent years an unfortunate trend in the United States and other free nations has been the tendency of many to talk and demand rights and privileges with little concern for responsibility of the individual. Marches, riots, vandalism, increasing crime rates, littered highways and landscapes provide chilling evidence of reality. Studies among various levels of school-age children have indicated it is indeed difficult to change the habits of those reared in an irresponsible valueless environment. Destruction of property, vandalism, graffiti, and flagrant abuse of others becomes life's values. Over 2,000 years ago Plato offered an explanation for irresponsible behavior. He said, "If man's education is inadequate or bad, he becomes the most savage of all the products on earth."

Irresponsibility is the dominant reason many people are bypassed in promotional considerations—simply unwilling to pay the price with responsibility for their actions. That price is courage, common sense, ethics, self-reliance; also the stamina to work hard, to make tough decisions, and put forth maximum effort and long hours for achievement. Each time a project of any description is undertaken, someone must be assigned and held responsible for results. Action planning, discussed in Chapter 3 to support worthy projects, is based on six important factors—WHY, WHAT, HOW, WHO, WHERE, and WHEN. The "WHO" factor is for designating the person responsible for a specific job. In leadership roles it is appropriate to assign responsibility to others. However, the leader remains accountable for the actions of subordinates. Your identity as a productive worker, leader, parent, teacher, doctor, lawyer, politician, or any other role will shine like a 1,000-watt bulb as you assume total responsibility for your actions.

Quality is fostered by responsible people.

Work Smarter, Not Harder

Are your activities and efforts organized?

During your active working life you will work approximately 100,000 hours. The accomplishments in this period of time will depend on two factors: Your attitude toward work and the manner in which you organize your efforts and allocate your time. Everyone has the same amount of time each day, 24 hours or 1,440 minutes, 168 hours per week. We cannot save time, but we can use it wisely. Many accomplish much with limited effort, some accomplish little with much effort. Many have an indifferent approach and achieve few of life's rewards. The difference can usually be attributed to the attitude toward activities and the manner in which they are organized.

"The meaning of man's work" suggested Paul Tournier "is the satisfaction of the instinct for adventure that God has implanted in his heart." Unfortunately, not everyone is happy in his work. When the pleasure of work is absent, output is affected, deliveries are slowed, production is low, costs go up and profits down. The person who enjoys his work is mentally absorbed and limitless energy seems to bubble forth. The challenge of work and life is exhilarating.

The conditions of the unhappy worker and the happy one are controllable since each creates the circumstances of his environment. One of two changes is necessary for the dissatisfied worker—change to a job that provides satisfaction or change the attitude toward the present job.

Economic pressures often become the master influence. Because of debts or limited job choice in a locale, a worker will spend a lifetime on a job for mere existence rather than seeking one that brings satisfaction. Much work has been done in recent years in behavioral science and occupational safety and health areas to help create a more favorable environment where poor economics and unpleasant work conditions prevail.

In my industrial studies of satisfied versus unsatisfied workers, I have found in general the contented worker is ambitious, has goals, is absorbed in extracurricular activities, pursues life to the fullest. The disenchanted worker transfers job attitude to other activities, has few goals, is not overly involved in community activities, seeks self-satisfying interests. It is the satisfied, quality-oriented worker who is anxious and willing to raise his achievement quotient. Good results generate the desire to do more and better work. The benefits that come from being a top performer creates momentum to push for higher plateaus.

Organized effort is usually goal-based. The productive person has given much thought to what he wants to achieve and has developed a plan to reach his goals.

Too, the organizer knows the value of time, has learned to set priorities, makes definitive plans, is willing to delegate work and set target dates for completion. Thus, time, priorities, plans, and delegation become key factors in managing work.

In the book *"Professionals At Their Best"* which I co-authored, I related a classic story of setting goals, priorities and planning work in an experience of Charles Schwab. While serving as President of Bethlehem Steel, he presented a consultant, Ivy Lee, with a challenging problem. "Show me a way to get more things done with my time and I'll pay you a fee." Lee gave Schwab a sheet of paper and said, "List the most important tasks you have to do tomorrow and number them in order of importance. Tomorrow, begin at once with No. 1 and stay with it until completed. Then, recheck your priorities and move to No. 2. Make this a habit each working day. When it works for you, give it to your staff. Try it as long as you like. Then send me a check for what you think it's worth."

In a few weeks, Schwab sent Lee a check for $25,000 with a note saying it was the most profitable lesson he had ever learned. Many time management programs are offered today. Most use a similar approach. I have patterned my time management plan after Lee's advice to Schwab and added personal refinements which I am pleased to pass along for your consideration.

My plan is to classify items such as mail, reports, and reading material into 1—2—3 priorities and label each accordingly. Then I prioritize the No. 1's into the most important and do them in sequence until completed. This is essentially what Schwab did. The No. 2's are treated in the same manner, but I don't waste time on them until the No. 1's are out of the way. There are occasional changes in priorities, usually brought about by another's priority awaiting your input. Those labeled No. 3 are put aside and receive no attention until No. 1s and No. 2s are finished. Some of the No. 3s are continually put aside and often the need fades (due to lack of value) and are discarded.

The value of prioritizing is in keeping high value projects moving and making the most of your time of 86,400 seconds per day. I heard it suggested that we should treat these seconds like an $86,400 daily withdrawal from life's bank account. At the end of each day write off as lost whatever you failed to invest for good purpose. If you fail to use the day's withdrawal, the loss is yours. There is no deposit of surplus in the bank, no drawing against the morrow. You must live in the present—on today's withdrawal. Invest it so as to generate the utmost in health, happiness, and success.

Some other time organizers I use are: Make it a practice to minimize paper shuffling—take definite action on each item to dispose or classify while it is in hand. Magazines and publications are handled in the same manner. Read selectively of pertinent articles rather than trying to read everything. Don't let magazines pile up or nothing will be read—the problem mounts as the stack of publications mount.

I keep a daily "to do" list of priorities on a 3″ x 5″ card, and carry it in my shirt pocket. It is readily available for frequent reference, additions, or change. While unscheduled events do arise, it gives me a constant priority guide. Items are crossed off as completed. It is very satisfying to keep on top of major issues and see projects completed without stress and strain.

One other major time organizer; I train subordinates not to bring me problems without suggested solutions. This has two advantages: It helps the subordinate use his or her creative talents and develop; it focuses my attention on recommendations and not on time-consuming problems.

The person who achieves uses his time wisely. He does not let his time go unused. Organize your activities and your efforts—work smarter, not harder. You can raise your achievement quotient.

Quality is the trademark of organized effort.

Build a Results-Oriented Reputation

Are you a results getter?
People who have recorded significant achievements or reached notable levels of success are often referred to as "people at the top." They reached that pinnacle primarily because they sought positive results through planned action.

We often read or hear of various classifications of people

such as "wonders," "watchers," "makers." The wonderers are those who stand around trying to figure out what's happening; the watchers are the curious observers, some criticizing or asking, "why this?"; the makers are the leaders out front with goals and action plans in mind paving the way—making things happen. Speaker, author, and friend, Cavett Robert says a maker is:

A creator of circumstance—not a creature.
Things don't happen to him, he happens to things.
He is the cause, not the result.
People are his opportunity, not his frustration.

Reverend Bob Schuller, also a popular speaker and author, classifies people in three categories: "Drop-Outs," "Hold-Outs," and "All-Outs." Obviously, the "All-Outs" are the ones who perform, are results oriented and top producers.

Webster defines productive as "having the quality or power of producing; bringing forth or able to bring forth in abundance effective results." I have found four dominant characteristics common among achievers. These are: Desire, Commitment, Willingness, and Dedication.

DESIRE is the starting point. Nothing great was ever accomplished without an internal burning catalyst that says, "This is what I want to do," "I can be successful," "I will reach the top." Desire is the foundation of goals and plans; the pacesetter, source of motivation. It unleashes personality traits that contribute to high productivity: persistence, judgment, independence, disciplined work habits.

COMMITMENT is the mental guidance system that sets priorities to keep you on course. It serves to generate internal momentum. It's like the battery in your car, or electric circuit in your home. When engaged, the car starts and moves forward; the house lights burn and modern appliances turn. Without commitment you are like a child learning to ride a new bicycle. You fall repeatedly until you gain momentum.

WILLINGNESS to share the fruits of your efforts motivates others to help. It's very difficult, virtually impossible for anyone to reach the top alone. Team effort is essential and team spirit is the spark that ignites the will in willingness. Everyone likes to be involved with a winner. They especially like to say, "I gave a helping hand."

DEDICATION to a purpose, cause, organization, or party, motivates people to excel. When those aspiring to get results and reach the top remain dedicated to their goals, they feel compelled to do their best.

You can build a reputation for achieving quality results. Be a maker, an all-outer, a results getter. Join the productive people who have a desire to achieve, are committed to goals and action plans, possess a sharing sensitivity, and are dedicated to the organization's purpose.

Quality personifies the results-oriented person.

Give Generous Measures

Do you give unselfishly of your talents and abilities?

Centuries ago Solomon wrote in Proverbs 11:24–25, "It is possible to give away and become richer! It is also possible to hold on too tightly and lose everything. Yes, the liberal man shall be rich! By watering others he waters himself."

The world loves a generous giver. It need not be money. In fact, many philanthropic gifts of money and material possessions such as art and jewels receive very little publicity. But the giver of talents and abilities in service to others is publicized and applauded for years.

A story is told about two women serving customers at a candy counter. The customers were mostly children, some accompanied by parents. It seemed strange that most of the customers wanted to be served by one clerk and not the other. On closer observation, the reason became apparent. The lady serving only a few customers would overfill the scales with candy, then take pieces off to reach the correct measure. The lady serving many customers would under-fill the scales with candy, then gently add pieces to reach the correct measure. The eye of the beholder was judge. Even though the measures given by both clerks were the same, the assumed generosity of one clerk influenced the buyers.

This same approach to serving people is repeated daily by many clerks and those in other roles. The process of persuading people to act by making them feel good is the very essence of our existence. It is the balance that gives stability to our economic system and to life itself. The generous giver is watering others as he waters himself. People are his opportunity, not his frustration.

You possess a reservoir of resources that await sharing with others. They are labeled talents and abilities. Their roots are anchored in the fountain of your resources—physical, mental, social, spiritual. Have you ever watched an actor or actress, singer or musician, return for a curtain call? The applause of the audience generated an encore, and then another. To justify the encore, the performers gave of their best and it was appreciated. So the audience shows their appreciation and they too are rewarded. Note that appreciation and reward is flowing in two directions. Note also that it was the God-given gifts of talents and abilities that set the "giving" cycle in motion.

"The generous heart is a happy heart," wrote Ida Scott Taylor. "If you have beautiful thoughts, why should you hoard them? If you have wonderful gifts, why should you hide them? If you have a warm, loving hand, why should you close it instead of opening it in cordial greeting? One little act of generosity is a small thing, yet you cannot perform the most trivial task which will be some blessing to someone else without being benefited by it yourself."

It costs no more to give generous measures; not in material things, but those ingredients that measure competence and represent quality. Yes! Your competence is measured in many ways. But few measures have more impact on those who judge than the manner in which you serve and work with or help others grow. Material possessions are the ploy of thieves and deserve your protection. Giving of yourself is a gift that will enhance your relationship and stature. Your achievement quotient will rise accordingly. Friends, co-workers, and others are ready to applaud and reward a generous performer.

Quality harbors the gifts of generous hands.

Adapt to Changes

Do you adjust quickly to innovations?

It seems we are always trying to get our house or business in shape so that we will not have to make any changes, although it is doubtful that will ever happen. New designs, new products are a fact of life. Changes do occur so fast in virtually every field that it is difficult to keep informed. The manager, leader, or achiever in any endeavor must adapt to change quickly to remain in the classification of "competent." Why? The consumers of products, people, are a market craving for and absorbing innovations that appear to make life more satisfying and enjoyable.

Seeing an old friend for the first time in twenty years the greeting was typical: "You haven't changed a bit." That's a nice way of saying, "Gee, you have aged and put on weight, especially around the waistline, but I would rather not tell you so." We know we change with years, but it is the acceptance of change that separates the achiever from those who prefer stagnation. Consider the typical steps to stagnation:

We've never done it that way.
We're not ready for that.

We're doing all right without it.
We've tried that once before.
We don't have the time.
That is not our responsibility.
It just won't work.

A simple statement which President Herbert Hoover recorded has permanent wisdom: "If we are going to accomplish anything in our time we must approach our problem in the knowledge that there is nothing rigid or immutable in human affairs. History is a story of growth, decay, and change."

Change involves the discovery of different methods of reaching a goal or objective. "There are twenty ways of going to a point" suggested Emerson "and one is the shortest, but set out at once on one. A man who has the presence of mind which can bring to him instantly all he knows, is worth a dozen men who know as much but can only bring it to light slowly."

The achiever is an innovator. Do not pursue change for the sake of change, rather change for the sake of improvement of an end result, whether it be cost, marketability of a product, an academic course, or other item. I recommend all changes be approached slowly to insure the alternate method is proven better and for acceptance by others.

There is a common belief that people resist change, but this is a false notion. Consider the acceptance of new cars, new appliances, different hair and clothing styles. People don't resist change. They resist being changed without some involvement or awareness. Most like to have something to say about changes that affect them. This is only natural. You probably feel the same way. "The art of progress is to preserve order amid change and to preserve change amid order," is an appropriate maxim.

In technical fields it is important to modify and change one's ideas as technology advances. Consider the phenomenal changes in the computer field in a few years. Technology has advanced from a massive, intricate black box of limited capacity that only a few understood to the homestyle desk model of chips and discs that store thousands upon thousands of memory characteristics. These changes have propelled other changes in all related technology from space travel and guided missiles to instant worldwide TV and telephone communications via satellites.

Here are five useful steps to consider as you evaluate changes you may wish to implement or those that may be thrust upon you:

1. Be willing to modify your efforts to reach a particular goal or objective when there is potential for improvement. Recognize that history is growth, decay, change. You are making history each passing moment.
2. Seek suggestions and/or confirmation about changes from people who can assist you in resolving and evaluating new ideas. Involvement by others reduces resistance to change.
3. Avoid stagnation thinking and shun those who are prone to think negatively.
4. Approach change slowly to insure alternate methods will work and, if necessary, will be accepted by others.
5. Avoid anxiety, stress, and strain when changes are in process or thrust upon you. Relax and evaluate the benefits. Look for the seeds of success in every change and build on them.

Sound advice is contained in a verse by Reinhold Niebuhr:

> God, grant me the serenity
> To accept the things I cannot change;
> The courage to change the things I can;
> And the wisdom to know the difference.

Quality evolves through change to reach standards of excellence.

Go an Extra Mile

Do you enjoy giving extra effort for others?
Mark Twain enjoyed telling people that his name was in the Bible. He referred, of course, to the oft-quoted passage from the Sermon On The Mount: "And whosoever shall compel thee to go a mile, go with him twain." The depth of meaning in this statement is considered one of the best approaches to competence and good human relationships. There are few other single bits of advice that convey more people power.

Successful people are not great achievers because of the position they hold but because of what they are. The power to achieve is a human quality of character: confidence, patience, persistence, concern for others. Since a person is totally dependent on people to help him climb the ladder of achievement, isn't it logical that the more help given to others the more help and rewards will be returned?

We live in an era of the forty-hour work week or less and numerous community functions that absorb extra time. The incentive to go an extra mile for employers or other people may seem dimmer today, but the payoff is as valid as it was on the delivery of that greatest of all sermons.

Extra effort in behalf of your employer or community is an act of initiative. It is a demonstration of interest in the job, the company or community, and its people. Managers are quick to notice initiative because it is a vital characteristic of leadership. It is a reflection of a good attitude toward a job and your personal future. Extra effort is, of course, exposing you to new knowledge, hence mental growth occurs. It serves to demonstrate greater confidence and loyalty. Too, it identifies you as a decisive person determined to grow and excel. This all adds up to recognition, promotion potential, and higher remuneration.

Extra effort in behalf of fellow employees, neighbors, community clubs, associations, and church has the same impact and payoff. While voluntary roles do not offer remuneration the progress through chairs of leadership in local clubs and associations is an equally important source of education and development. Thus, while you are helping yourself you are helping others by going an extra mile.

For reference, look again at some of the key benefits of extra effort:

- Demonstrates initiative
- Characterizes leadership
- Reflection of good attitude
- Exposure to new knowledge
- Demonstrates personal confidence
- Displays sense of loyalty
- Shows decisiveness and determination
- Identifies promotion potential

A tale that was written by Orison S. Marden told of a mighty king who had one little son whom he worshipped. The boy had everything he desired, all that wealth and love could give, but he was not happy. His face was always disfigured by a scowl of discontent. One day, a great magician came to the king's palace and told him he could make his son happy and turn his scowls into smiles. "If you can do this," said the king, "I will give you whatever you ask." The magician took the boy into a private chamber and wrote something with a white substance on a piece of paper. He gave the paper to the boy and told him to go into a darkened room and hold a lighted candle under it and see what would happen. Then the magician went away. The young prince did as he was instructed, and the white letters, illuminated by the light from beneath, turned into a beautiful blue and formed the words: "Do a kindness to someone every day." The prince followed the magician's advice and soon became the happiest boy in his father's kingdom.

By giving of himself and putting forth effort in his relations with people, the young man found new hope, joy, and satisfying rewards.

The aura of competence will not glow around you because of who you are or what you know. Oh sure, these things are important. But you are not your own judge. That providence rests in the eyes and feelings of those you serve. "If you want to be the greatest, you must first be the least, a servant of all," spoke the Master. Competence is comprised of many ingredients. High on the list is, "what you are," and "how much you care," in the eyes of your judges—those you serve. Go an extra mile for others and discover why Mark Twain also appreciated this wisdom of yesterday.

Quality and extra service to others rank supreme.

Keep Your Eyes on Finances

Do you possess money consciousness?
"The way to wealth is as plain as the way to market. It depends chiefly on two words, industry and frugality; that is, waste neither time nor money, but make the best use of both. Without industry and frugality, nothing will do; and with them everything," advised Benjamin Franklin. These words have stood the test of time. Earnings, lendings, borrowings, investments, and savings represent power or the lack of it. The entire free enterprise system, the stability of the nation revolves around the power of money.

Money will invariably seek the level of competence of the person controlling it, much as water will seek the level of its source. A man never rises above his own self-image and this vision is directly tied to thoughts and actions. Hence, your money resources will be stimulated to grow or diminish as a result of your industry and frugality.

Competence does not accrue to the person who is unable to manage finances successfully. Power does not flow to the one who cannot control it. Achievers in profit and nonprofit businesses must possess a keen sense of money consciousness. Managers may rely on financial advisors for day-to-day guidance on the flow of money in an enterprise, but they remain accountable for the results of the entity; hence they must tightly control money resources. A very high ratio of new business ventures fail in the first year due to unsound financial planning either in initial start-up or in methods of operation—a reflection on the financial competency and judgment of the founders.

Make sound financial management a primary goal in your personal and business life. Set up a system to control the money flowing through your fingers whether it be small or large sums. Any entity, including your home, needs a system for controlling money. Haphazard measures lead to carelessness, overextending credit, and loss of buying or negotiating power. The system should always include a budget of expenditures based on income or available funds.

A primary key to personal growth and competence is the habit of saving and investing. Savings and investment capital represent power. Let's be candid. There is no negotiating power when dealing from indebtedness beyond your means. The real power is in what you possess. To ignore a system that builds power is to shun competence. Financial power or energy needs to be harnessed or put into a system to engender competence, confidence, and a strong self-image.

In the book, *The Land That God Gave Cain,* J. M. Scott writes about an expedition to Labrador by dog teams. He describes three systems for harnessing sledge dogs that pull large loads. In pairs or a single trace, in single file, or spread out in the shape of a fan. The fan system is the safest way on thin ice because there is little danger of all the dogs going through the ice at the same time. But the weight of several different traces creates a problem in the fan. The traces become entangled and it is necessary to stop traveling every hour or so to unwind them. Dogs at the side are not getting a direct pull on the sledge, thus energy power is wasted.

A system for control of money flow is like a harness. Your choice of systems vary from a piece of paper to a computer. As with the dog sledges, it is important that you adopt the system that gives you the most power or energy with the money in your sledge cargo. The absence of effective control may put you on thin ice with little competence.

I recommend taking definite steps to keep atop finances. As a minimum, the following suggestions will put you on solid footing:

1. Make financial knowledge an insatiable curiosity. Awareness of power through money resources is a giant step toward competence. Let common sense be your guide in using money to build a solid future.
2. Make financial management a primary goal in your personal and business life. It will pay off in personal growth as rapidly as you reflect your competence and understanding in dealing with money matters.
3. Adopt a system of control that includes a sound budget based on income and available funds. The budget should include a ratio for savings and investments.
4. Establish a personal goal for savings and investment. Let savings be a favorite habit that must be satisfied. Put something into the plan regularly and it will become a habit. "Big oaks from little acorns grow," is a worthy ancient proverb.
5. Build a genuine interest and concern for spending in government and civic programs. Use your financial awareness to influence common sense controls and frugality in all areas.
6. Consider money a means to an end, not an end in itself. Manage it wisely. Spend or invest it with common sense. Follow the admonition of Benjamin Franklin— pursue industry and frugality.

Quality results demonstrate industrious habits and frugality.

Develop Subordinates

Are you preparing for higher plateaus?
Constantly striving for something better is the price of progress. Competition is a driving force that motivates man to reach for higher plateaus. The surest way to progress

and to compete for greater rewards is to develop followers or subordinates. And, concurrently, to develop yourself through exposure to new knowledge and experience.

The chances of making substantial progress in a job or program, being selected for promotion or for another job, will be influenced by two key factors: The competence and performance of subordinates; the candidates available to take your place. Today's well-managed enterprises implement appropriate training and career-development programs for their employees to insure progress. Well-managed professional sports teams train extensively. They carry trained second and third level reserves, and also support farm teams as a continuing source of talent.

In my recruiting experience for industry and business the majority of applications to fill key manager roles were a result of management's failure to develop qualified people already in their employ. The development of subordinates is a management responsibility to help foster the growth of an entity, its employees or members. Growth of a company, club, or association will follow the development of its people. The absence of development opportunities will be reason for people to seek more progressive challenges elsewhere.

The training and development of subordinates is not something to be treated lightly. Machiavelli said in *The Prince,* "The first opinion which one forms of a prince, and of his understanding, is by observing the men he has around him." If you fail to develop your subordinates two handicaps result: mediocre talent restricts entity growth and profitability to the level of their knowledge and skill; mediocre minds will not contribute to your progress or become replacement candidates.

Competence is seldom, if ever, the result of a single effort. It is a result of the outpouring on many who join in a common venture to generate quality in which all can reflect pride. Leaders who mold and shape competent followers raise themselves to a higher level of competence. To elevate your achievement quotient make it a prime responsibility to develop subordinates by sowing seeds of knowledge and experience. And sow an ample quantity of seeds for your own personal development. The reward will be represented by an abundant harvest and personal progress. In the words of Goethe:

We must not hope to be mowers
And to gather the ripe gold ears,
Unless we have first been sowers
And watered the furrows with tears.

It is not just as we take it
The mystical world of ours,
Life's field will yield as we make it
A harvest of thorns or of flowers.

Quality must be sown before it can be harvested.

Practice the Golden Rule

Do you treat others as you wish to be treated?
A class of college students pursuing the study of human relations was asked: "Is there a single word that might serve as a rule for the practice of good human relations?" Hours of search and discussion were spent trying to identify and agree on a single word. There did not seem to be one word that encompassed this vast subject. Then one student said "let's consider the golden rule, and see if we can find a single word that best describes it." The students found a Bible and read the words from Matthew 7:12, "Whatsoever ye would that men should do to you, do you even so to them." The word search continued like a game of scrabble. Finally one student said, "I think I've got it—would the word 'reciprocity' fit?" "Yes," the students agreed. "An exchange of mutual rights and privileges, mutual giving and receiving, giving and taking."

139

The simplicity of this rule and the single word reciprocity provokes most people to look for other ideas. It just cannot be that easy. But it is. There are volumes of books and papers written on human relations, how to get along with people and how to treat mankind. "Reciprocity," that's it! But most will continue the endless search, pursue more complex analyses, and offer more equally complex solutions.

For more than four thousand years this rule has been preached to Christians. Similar rules are contained in other religious doctrines. While intended as a standard of conduct for men, few, it seems, have understood its deep significance. Man is the shaper of his own destiny. We have discussed that in earlier chapters. Now we read it again in divine simplicity and it's hard to accept—"Whatsoever a man soweth that shall he also reap." Thus, walking over people to satisfy personal ambitions leads to destruction of relationships. It tears down the very source of energy which people provide for you to be a competent achiever. Walking with people and reciprocating mutual rights and privileges builds strength and support to reach out for higher pinnacles.

Human relations never seem to be what they could be. Simple guidelines are hard to apply. The world of people is beset by wars and threats of wars, crimes, greed, strife, hunger, and other miseries. All are attributable to human failings. All reflect on the incompetence of man to deal fairly with fellow human beings.

But human relations can be what you want them to be. It is your destiny at stake. You are the builder. The rule is in your hands. The word reciprocity is now in your vocabulary. Your achievement level will be as high as your personal standards will allow—no higher. Therefore, let competence be your goal and reciprocity in human relations your standard.

As you apply the golden rule consider the sound advice of Charles Dickens: "Try to do to others as you would have them do to you and do not be discouraged if they fail sometimes. It is much better that they should fail than that you should."

Quality is the standard of competent people.

In the achievement formula quality is a standard of highest order and reflects your degree of competence in all things. Consider again the principal points in each section, also the apothegms and let them serve as your guide as you reach for a higher achievement quotient:

1. Competence power is like a light bulb. The light is dependent on the strength of its elements. Man's output power is also dependent on the elements that comprise his total ability.
2. Education and development is a lifelong process. Build on your knowledge and skills, also shape your attitude to take advantage of new opportunities. Your only limitations are those which are self-imposed.
3. The price of personal growth is responsibility for your own actions. Life's ladder of achievement is predicated on willingness to assume rungs of responsibility—"I can," "I will," "I did."
4. All people are given the same amount of time, that is, 1440 minutes or 24 hours each day, 168 hours each week. It cannot be saved, but it can be used wisely. Invest your time so as to generate the utmost in health, happiness, and success.
5. Creators of circumstance become achievers because of their ability to produce effective results. Dominant characteristics of results-oriented people are: Desire; Commitment; Willingness to share; Dedication to a purpose, cause, organization.
6. The generous heart is a happy heart. The giver of talents and abilities in service to others is a label of unselfishness and desire.
7. Be receptive to change. Avoid stagnation and negativism. History is a story of growth, decay, and change.
8. Going an extra mile for others creates an unmistakable image of initiative and good attitude. It identifies your standards and values.
9. The ability to manage your personal and job-related finances

is a mark of competence. Make saving and investing a habit for building money power.

10. The surest way to progress and to compete for greater rewards is to develop followers or subordinates. Also, to develop yourself through exposure to new knowledge and experience.

11. Make the Golden Rule a part of your life. Remember the word "reciprocity"—an exchange of mutual rights and privileges, mutual giving and receiving, giving and taking—and practice it.

APOTHEGMS

1. *Quality is founded in the desire and commitment to excel.*
2. *Quality is fostered by responsible people.*
3. *Quality is the trademark of organized effort.*
4. *Quality personifies the results-oriented person.*
5. *Quality harbors the gifts of generous hands.*
6. *Quality evolves through change to reach standards of excellence.*
7. *Quality and extra service to others rank supreme.*
8. *Quality results demonstrate industrious habits and frugality.*
9. *Quality must be sown before it can be harvested.*
10. *Quality is the standard of competent people.*

9
Personality Power

Ideals are like stars. You will not succeed in touching them; but, like the seafaring man, you choose them as your guides and, following them, you will reach your destiny.

—Carl Schurz

(DELIVERY)

This chapter is the beginning of another stimulating voyage to five ports of call along the journey of DELIVERY. It is the third of the three factors in the Achievement Quotient formula multiplier, C (P + Q + D) = AQ.

Do you portray a magnetic personality?

The delivery of one's talents and abilities, either directly or through a tangible product, is considered the most significant factor of the multipliers. While all three factors are of utmost importance, the buyer of goods and services is always responsive to the delivery system. Of particular importance is the method of delivery and the treatment by those who handle the product. Method includes the source, convenience, display, attractiveness, packaging, and similar factors. Treatment includes the behavior of those who sell, serve, and deliver; their kindness, respect, care, helpfulness, and follow-up service. This combination of many factors represents the total delivery system and is a reflection of one's personality or that of the organization represented.

Personality is the basic architecture of life. It displays your attitude toward all things. It identifies the values you possess and share with others. The most important function of your education at any level is to develop your personality so as to effectively utilize and dispense acquired knowledge and skill. Educators throughout the centuries have agreed that the primary objective of education is to attain an integration of the personality with knowledge. Without acquiring this internal harmony, knowledge is of limited value.

Author Edith Joynson offers us a vivid description of an attractive personality in these words: "An appealing personality is not something grafted on from without. It is not like a coat of paint applied to a building or cosmetics used on the face. It is expressed through the body, the mind, the heart, and the spirit. Although some persons seem to have been born with an exceptionally appealing personality, no one has a monopoly on it."

A magnetic personality, one that attracts people to share your life, is an asset of ever-increasing value. Properly controlled, it can propel you to heights beyond your imagination. People will willingly help boost you to new horizons because of what you are.

The essence of personality is found in attitude toward life and toward other people. It is not something that can be purchased. But, like love, it can be developed and serve to greatly enhance your achievement quotient. The chapter sections that follow will explore useful steps that you can pursue as you seek to develop this valueless trait—personality power.

Magnify Your Potential

Are you developing your personality?
The successful delivery of goods and services, talents and abilities, is tied closely to personality. There is no question

that the person displaying a magnetic personality has the best potential for growth. An aura of personal attractiveness magnifies one's possibilities many times. Your personality is the sum total of those characteristics that distinguish you from others. They reflect your attitude, self-esteem, and values in life. These traits can be polished so as to maximize your strengths and improve weaknesses depending on your perceived needs and desires. Since the needs and interests of people are many and varied, it would be impractical if not impossible, to offer a menu of personality development suggestions from which to pick and choose. However, I shall suggest several steps that can serve to enhance your potential.

The values set forth in Chapter 1, "Humanity Power," are all relevant to personality development. It would be worthy to reread that chapter for full appreciation of the impact of your personality on people relations.

The starting point of all improvement plans is personal desire which, of course, you must initiate. You must sincerely and intently want to develop certain traits to enhance your growth potential. If the plan is to be considered worthy, it should be preceded by a written goal. Then specific steps can be pursued to polish strengths and improve weaknesses. These, of course, would be described in the action plan format outlined in Chapter 3. Now that we are on track, consider the following suggestions:

Appearance: The clothes you wear, hair style, cleanliness, posture, walk, and facial characteristics identify your personality and life style. These factors should depict the direction you are headed and the role you expect to play. Study your goals; consider modifying those factors that may be obstacles or need improvement.

Vitality: People like to join the person who exhibits physical exuberance, an energetic spark, a spirit or life force that is destined to go places. A healthy outlook on life as well as a healthy positive self-assured approach to work and social activities attracts others.

Voice: Pleasantries come in many ways, but a friendly

well-modulated voice will gain a listening ear quickly. Loud, boisterous voice and unpolished grammar turns people off.

Listening: The good communicator is a good listener. Avoid appearing aloof or uninterested in others. Cultivate good listening habits to enhance your personality image.

Eyes: Expressiveness of the eyes are a reflection of your moods, sincerity, warmth, friendliness. Develop the habit of looking into the eyes of others as you talk or meet them— looking away denotes lack of interest or concern.

Kinesics: Body actions, the silent messages conveyed, are very meaningful—they should reflect the intent of your words and be equally expressive.

Handshake: This accepted method of welcoming or greeting is another expression of feelings; warmth, friendship, and desire to be associated with others. The absence of it is a serious reflection against your personality—it connotes coolness, aloofness and desire to avoid rather than join others. A firm handshake will be interpreted as warm and friendly. The weak, slovenly handshake connotes a weak, disinterested personality.

Participation: Get involved with others; build new relationships; expand your circle of contacts. Each contact provides an opportunity to extend your knowledge and your relationships. Additionally, it is motivating and inspiring to be with others. New associations will strengthen personality development.

Emotions: Control your own emotional reactions to situations such as arguments and disagreements. A level head attracts followers. A hothead usually walks alone or in company with like personalities.

The suggestions for building a more attractive personality can play an important role as you pursue improvement in your achievement quotient. Since achievement is, of course, influenced by those with whom you work or associate, then relationship becomes a potent force. Hence, personality growth and achievement growth go hand in hand.

As you pursue the study of improving your personality

power and its impact on others, don't expect miraculous changes overnight. Whatever habits or traits that you want to change were probably acquired over a lengthy period. The same habit force will make the desired changes for you now. But first, set your goals and pursue them daily with the intent of growing a little each day.

Delivery with a winning personality fosters personal growth.

Radiate Your Personality

Do you wear a sunny disposition?

The ratio of people who want to associate with you, share your interests, buy your goods and services, enjoy your talents and abilities, will be in proportion to the radiance of your personality. Of all the human characteristics which your body, mind, and actions convey, the friendliness and warmth of your smile is the most powerful.

More audiences have been won over by the happy disposition of speakers, actors, sales personnel, leaders, than the words that were spoken. A captivating countenance is of inestimable value. An unpleasant, cold, sourly disposed approach to life can lead to a lonely, unsatisfying, unproductive existence.

Your personality is reflected through the sincerity of your facial expression, magnified by the confidence of a stern set chin, the breadth and warmth of a friendly smile. "Nothing on earth can smile but man! Gems may flash reflected light, but what is a diamond-flash compared to an eye-flash and a mirth-flash? Flowers cannot smile; this is a charm that even they cannot claim. It is the prerogative of man; it is the color which love wears, and cheerfulness and joy— these three. It is a light in the windows of the face by which the heart signifies it is at home and waiting. A face that cannot smile is like a bud that cannot blossom, and dries up to the stalk. Laughter is day, and sobriety is night, and

a smile is the twilight that hovers gently between both—
more bewitching than either," advised Henry Ward Beecher.

The next time you walk down the sidewalk of a crowded
busy street, look into the faces of the passersby. You will
doubtless see a mass of fixed stares instead of smiles. Stop
then and think about your own facial mode. It too will be
a frozen expression of unconcern for the world around you.
Now put on a smile and walk further and notice the friendly
smiles and nodding heads. Your radiance will prove contagious. Take this lesson home, to the job, and everywhere
you travel. In a brief period of time you will discover the
pleasure of helping others enjoy life by wearing a happy
expression. Abraham Lincoln remarked, "Most folks are
about as happy as they make up their minds to be," and
he was right. You can help people change their minds by
wearing the radiance of a smile on your face.

Courage, like a smile, is contagious. In any crisis, people
look to their leader for courage. If the leaders are courageous,
followers will pursue the example. During my involvement
in World War II, there were a number of close encounters
that tested one's courage to keep moving forward. Fear was
difficult to avoid when dangers and the hazards of bombs,
guns, and other explosives were flying and falling. When
the leader reflected an unsmiling, but determined expression,
dangers were quite evident. But when the news of safe waters
and clear shores was evident smiles of winning or holding
ground were a sufficient message to generate more strength
and move forward with confidence.

Sales personnel are usually taught to appreciate that a
sale is half made when a customer is greeted with a smile.
It is easy to deal with the person who depicts a friendly
face and helpful disposition. Prices, quality, and other factors
seem less important when the salesperson reflects confidence
and a smile. There is an immediate aura of trust and belief
that overshadows doubt about a product or service.

Virtually every successful sales group pursues a creed;
usually these are memorized as a stimulus to good customer

relations. While many such creeds are adopted, I have not read one that did not focus heavily on the value of a smile and good mental attitude. Excerpts from an-oft quoted creed written by Wilferd A. Peterson on the "Art of Getting Along," says:

> I believe that pleased customers are my greatest asset.
> I believe in the radiant power of a smile.
> I believe in the victorious mental attitude.
> I believe that my success is up to me.

Morale of people is of great importance to productivity. Whether we stop to think about it or not, each of us is conscious at all times of the state of morale among any group with which we are associated. Morale is engendered largely as a result of mental attitude, hope, and confidence. It is sustained by spirit and pride that prevails among the group.

The key lies in our approach to life and our individual attitude. Morale is a condition that we generate, like happiness and good feelings. The radiance of a confident personality can do more to lift and sustain good morale than any words. A smile is a reflection of confidence. You may not smile because you are cheerful, but you will be cheerful because you smile.

Delivery with a smile is a bridge to friendship.

Become a Good Conversationalist

Do you generate conversation with ease?

A college professor was asked by a student: "Is there anything I can do to learn the art of conversation?" "Yes, there is one thing," replied the professor. "If you will listen I will tell you." There was silence for several moments. "I'm listening," said the student. "You see," responded the professor, "you are learning already."

149

In conducting seminars on attitudinal development, I ask participants to list the names of three or four people they feel are good listeners. Invariably the names listed are close relatives or friends. Those with whom we can share intimate thoughts without fear of reprisal or embarrassment are our favorite conversationalists. But it is their willing listening interest and seldom their conversation that attracts. The maxim" a friend is a speaking acquaintance who also listens" is an apt description.

Business and social activities are influenced by the desire of people to share your interests and awareness. The type of personality that you project thus becomes the crossroads to higher achievement. The road you select to project your personality can attract or repel people. Hence, it is important to assess the personality you now present versus that which you should project to maximize personal warmth, sincerity, and growth. Ask yourself: "How do I come through to people?" It is often helpful to seek impartial, unbiased advice on how you come through to others in conversation, then work to improve the areas that justify change. Consider the following personality types:

Introvert —moody, happy to be alone, brooder.
Extrovert —good mixer, outgoing, interested in external things, show off.
Ambivert —some elements of both an introvert and extrovert.
Egocentric —self-centered, selfish, indifferent to others' interests.
Inhibited —restrained, conservative, fears ridicule.
Exhibitionist—show off, hogs the spotlight, a spectacle.
Diffident —bashful, modest, timid, hesitant.
Effervescent—bubbling over with zest, happy, sparkling.
Gregarious —fond of the company of others, sociable.

The personality of many might be described by several of the above words. For example, the extrovert may also be an exhibitionist at times; the introvert may reflect inhibitions or diffidence.

The good conversationalist is most likely to be the gregarious type who is fond of company. This type radiates an effervescence or friendliness through his body actions and facial expressions—a smile and sparkling eyes. Too, they might be classed as ambivalent, possessing some elements of an introvert and extrovert.

Conversation has five main purposes. To give, get, or exchange information; to persuade and to share interests with others. Good conversation stretches your mind even if no worthwhile conclusions are reached. "Man's mind stretched to a new idea, never goes back to its original dimension," said Oliver Wendell Holmes. But to make the most of any exchange conversation should be viewed as a mental occupation, not merely wheel-spinning or words about nothing. We shall now explore some steps that you can pursue to expand your conversational strengths and, in turn, influence achievement:

1. DESIRE is the starting point for any change. Conversation consists of both speaking and listening. While there are no rules of order per se, the reflection of sincere interest in others is the primary door opener. This, coupled with politeness, is a setting for a pleasurable experience. Approach conversation with the idea of drawing people closer to you and not trying to hold them spellbound.

2. DIALOGUE is conversation with a purpose to achieve useful results. The nations of the world revolve around discussions and exchange of dialogue among leaders. Business and its many facets could not survive without discussion, deliberation, negotiation. Recognize that dialogue with people is essential in all of life's active roles. It is the basis for creative thought, the builder of ideas, the shaper of destiny. While silence is sometimes golden, the achiever pursues conversation with

purpose—the intended results need not be for gain or some selfish motive; they can be sheer enjoyment.

3. PUT OTHERS FIRST as you seek to generate conversation. Nearly everyone is anxious to tell others about their hobbies, jobs, families, travels. By putting others first you not only attract others, you also learn something about them—your circle of awareness is enlarged. To listen brings into the open a mass of experience and incidents that broadens your own perspective of life.

4. BE IMPARTIAL to points of view. This is a valued aid in rendering sound judgments about the subject under discussion and gives you the freedom of drawing unbiased conclusions. Many irritations and disagreements occur because of biased views. An open mind generates healthy conversation. The closed mind leads to disagreement. While you may oppose a person's view, always endeavor to see things through the other person's eyes for their awareness is probably more or less than your own.

5. PLAN AHEAD as you approach business or social meetings. Anticipate the environment and the joy of making people your opportunity, not your frustration. Go prepared to generate conversation with others. Plan to consciously put others first and to pursue impartial dialogue. I do not mean to overlook the typical enjoyment of kidding, leg-pulling, good-time personal exchange. These events occur in most friendly crowds and are the fun side of life—do not overlook the joy of humorous and playful exchange. Laughter is the music of the soul. But have fun conversation when appropriate and stick to business when the atmosphere calls for business. Be wise enough to know the difference.

6. STICK TO THE SUBJECT to generate worthwhile conversation. Dialogue is seeking the truth. It involves the willingness to seek understanding which may not be clear to those involved. Small problems within a

large picture call for clarity to avoid disaster. No solution is complete without consideration of the internal elements. It is easy to identify the uninterested in any dialogue—they are always starting side conversations and leading others astray. This is suicide in business meetings of any type. Always show respect for others' knowledge and their role in the subject under discussion.

7. AVOID PROFANITY as it reveals your level of intellect and size of your vocabulary. My father once advised, "Son, only an uneducated nit without a respectable vocabulary substitutes with profane words. When you hear someone expound their thoughts with profanity it only means they don't know enough words to speak intelligently. Son, you can either sound stupid or intelligent—which will it be?" I got the message. From that day to this I have preferred to sound intelligent and avoid the words that connote stupidity.

8. MAKE YOURSELF A JOY TO BE WITH and your level of achievement will continue to rise. Whatever your role in life or your goal, the open, friendly, gregarious personality attracts people like a magnet. This image is a result of being a good conversationalist—one who is always a good listener with an insatiable interest in people. Analyze your present traits, the pluses and minuses. Consider those factors that may be holding you back. They can be improved. You can become an interesting conversationalist. Put your best foot forward and draw others to you with a warm personality, open mind, and the desire to be a joy to others.

Delivery success rides the waves of harmonious dialogue.

Make Lasting Impressions

Do you help others fulfill their ego needs?

The ability to impress and get along well with people is a prime attribute in any venture. The degree to which you can successfully persuade others to partake of your wares depends to a great degree on their impressions of you, the confidence you generate, and how you support and reinforce their actions.

Psychologists have long advocated that the deepest urge in human nature is "the desire to be important." In work, social, and other activities you deal with men and women who have feelings of pride and satisfaction, possess the ambition to achieve, and the desire for love and affection. They are responsive to the same psychological needs as yourself. People are, of course, different in heredity and experiences. These similarities and differences are the basis for study as you seek to extend your understanding and relations with people.

Will full appreciation of the fact that people do desire to feel or be important, it will be easy for you to see the value of a warm, caring, friendly personality. I do not encourage this viewpoint to selfishly magnify your own ego. That will come in abundance as a result of your relations with others. "Give and you shall receive" is the intended approach. It is not receive and then give.

Many virtues prevail, but four are significant as you seek to impress and build rapport and work successfully with people. They are: consistency, integrity, sincerity, and friendliness. People are quick to recognize inconsistent and phony behavior. Lack of sincerity can be detected in so many ways, such as in the voice, eyes, body actions. It is foolish to present a false front in hopes it will not be noticed or felt. These four virtues are usually evident in your face whether or not you communicate vocally. In the poetic words of an unknown author:

You don't have to tell how you live each day;
You don't have to say if you work or you play;
A tried, true barometer serves in its place,
However you live, it will show in your face.

The false and deceit that you bear in your heart
Will not stay inside where it first got its start;
For sinew and blood are a thin veil of lace,
What you wear in your heart, you wear in your face.

If your life is unselfish, if for others you live,
For not what you get, but how much you can give;
If you live close to God in His infinite grace,
You don't have to tell it, it shows in your face.

Yes, people feel more secure in their relationship with leaders and others who deal in a consistent unselfish manner. Consistency and unselfishness breeds harmony among people and the desire to work together. People want to do business with those who make them feel worthy, important, and comfortable. Therefore, actions that belittle or create discomfort are like striking the wrong note on the piano scale; discord exists immediately.

Integrity is a reflection of character, moral principles, honesty, good faith, respectability, loyalty. The constant pursuit of fairness and reinforcement given others is like a magnet. People are drawn close because of the way they conduct themselves, and the way you treat them. They see you for what you are, not what you know, want, or possess.

Sincerity is significant because it depicts an attitude of mind, a trusting supportive relationship. It requires cultivation and acceptance in business and social circles. Differences of opinion will occur from time to time. However, when sincerity and a supportive and trusting relationship prevail, freedom to discuss and work out problems in an amicable manner will also exist.

Friendliness reflects an internal feeling and spirit of mutual respect. True friendship radiates a warmth and supportive feeling that motivates you to oblige and work with others regardless who receives the benefit or credit. And, in turn, people are inspired to be with you.

All people have an insatiable ego that requires feeding

for their peace of mind and good feelings. Those with whom you work or associate will be influenced by the manner in which you support and reinforce their ego through praise, compliments, helpfulness, guidance, counsel. Reinforcement of others' actions is always most effective when offered for tangible progress or improvements, preferably something measurable and visible such as academic progress, achieving specific goals. Leave lasting impressions of confidence and humility by helping others feel good about themselves and their relationship with you. Your personality characterizes the charisma or lack of it that influences people relationships. It is an inestimable power source that gives harmony to life and, in turn, an ever-increasing achievement quotient.

Delivery charisma builds relationships of mutual and lasting benefit.

Avoid Making Enemies

Do your friends outnumber your enemies?

The higher a person rises in job responsibility the greater the number of boosters and friends. The one who rubs people the wrong way and develops a number of enemies will have little opportunity for growth. Enemies in business and social life are considered by some to be the inevitable result of competition for jobs, political office, and business. In reality, the majority of such dissidents are usually self-generated or imagined. Some personal jealousies and differences may exist. But the fewer the better.

To prove the above premise, observe key managers or community leaders who have been in business a few years. They will have an increasing number of followers. Their competence rather than failings will be the subject of discussion. Enemies, if any, will be those of little influence. Then observe managers or leaders who have been struggling for years with limited progress, often being passed over or subor-

dinated to lesser roles. They will have generated some enemies or at least feelings of dislike among people. A negative
attitude will have influenced several to dislike them without
even knowing them personally. People in higher roles will
not recommend them because of their personality or attitudinal approach to life.

When people are praised for their accomplishments, good
word gets around, sometimes slowly because most like to
see proof of excellence. But criticism of any kind, however
small, travels like wildfire to all circles. It becomes common
gossip in minutes. This perhaps accounts for the fact that
85 percent of communications centers on problems and failings of people. Only about 15 percent of our communications relate to rewards and recognition.

There are few people who can constantly walk the straight
and narrow without an occasional offense, sometimes unin-
tentional or without knowing an action was disturbing.
Achievers are usually highly motivated, aggressive people
pursuing opportunities to obtain results. Risks are often involved. The adventurous type is more apt to achieve beneficial rewards for pushing to the front. Mistakes will occur
and may generate dissidence among some, but the achiever
learns quickly from mistakes and turns them into opportunities for growth. Too, if offense occurs or an adversary is
created, the achiever will quickly mend the relationship and
continue making people his opportunity.

Enemies that you create are like a pimple on your face.
They are a source of constant irritation, reflect on your appearance, and occupy precious thought time that might be
devoted to productive effort.

Adversary relationships or enemies are usually conceived
in four ways: dishonesty, unfairness, threats, inflexibility.

1. DISHONESTY or cheating turns business and social
   relations sour quickly and often permanently. Honesty
   among business competitors does not create enemies.
   But dishonest competition and price fixing does. The

wise man looks on competition as cooperators, people pursuing the same cause and deserving of respect.

2. UNFAIRNESS or taking advantage of people is a devious act to satisfy selfish motives. Self-satisfaction at the expense of others destroys relationships and may lead to the courtroom.

3. THREATS, whether real or imagined are a senseless source of irritation that constantly absorb the mind of the offended. They will stew in the juice of the threat until it is resolved or receive an apology. Even the unintended abrasive comment arouses negative emotions and causes people to spread destructive gossip.

4. INFLEXIBILITY or the unbending desire to "have things my way" is merely placing untenable obstacles in the path of progress. Compromise and harmony among people will accrue more dividends than standing on the pride of one's convictions. Remember there will always be shades of differences in every circumstance. Few situations are precisely black or white.

Human relationships are a fragile commodity. Some dissidents or enemies are difficult to avoid. No one is free of jealous and pragmatic people. Often the opposed are unknown; some simply harbor secret dislikes. Occasional bad press will pop up for little or no apparent reason. But the fewer the number of dissidents along the way, the higher your achievement quotient will be.

Progress cannot be made walking on eggs. Solid footing is essential to move ahead. Consider enemies as obstacles to growth; cooperative people as stepping stones for achievement. Which will it be?

The words of Francis M. Balfour offer appropriate advice for many situations: "The best thing to give your enemy is forgiveness; to an opponent, tolerance; to a friend, your heart; to a child, a good example; to a father, deference; to your mother, conduct that will make her proud of you; to yourself, respect; to all men, charity."

Delivery power grows as followers join your purpose.

The importance of personality power in building an effective delivery system merits a thorough review of the key points in each chapter section. Too, the apothegms can serve as lifelong references of value:

1. Personality is the basic architecture of life. It is a reflection of your attitude. It identifies the values you possess and share with others. A magnetic personality can be developed; it is an asset of ever-increasing value.
2. For continued growth you must sincerely and intently want to develop traits that will magnify your potential.
3. Personality is reflected through the sincerity of your facial expression, magnified by the confidence of a stern set chin, the breadth and warmth of a smile. A smile is a reflection of confidence.
4. Business and social activities are influenced by the desire of people to share your interests and awareness. The good conversationalist is most likely to be the gregarious type who is fond of company.
5. Lasting impressions will occur to the extent that you satisfy the deepest urge in human nature, "the desire to be important." Four significant virtues will help you build rapport and work successfully with people: consistency, integrity, sincerity, and friendliness.
6. Avoid creating enemies; they will tear apart your dreams for achievement. Some personal jealousies and differences may exist. But the fewer the better. Enemies are obstacles to progress; cooperative people are stepping stones for achievement.

APOTHEGMS

1. *Delivery with a winning personality fosters personal growth.*
2. *Delivery with a smile is a bridge to friendship.*
3. *Delivery success rides the waves of harmonious dialogue.*
4. *Delivery charisma builds relationships of mutual and lasting benefit.*
5. *Delivery power grows as followers join your purpose.*

10
Enthusiasm Power

*Every great and commanding move-
ment in the anals of the world is the
triumph of enthusiasm. Nothing great
was ever achieved without it.*
—Ralph Waldo Emerson

(DELIVERY)

Are you excited about raising your AQ?

Emerson was right. Nothing great was ever achieved without enthusiasm. Your achievement level can grow to any desired height providing you have the enthusiasm to make it happen. It is the propelling power, the fuel that converts desire into action. It turns those who are just existing into being somebody with a purpose for living. It transforms perpetual losers into consistent winners, wonderers into makers, complacent into action people. The Psalmists must have thought of this ingredient in describing the blessed man in Psalm 1, "He shall be like a tree planted by the rivers of water, that bringeth forth his fruit in his season; his leaf also shall not wither, and whatsoever he doeth shall prosper."

Enthusiasm is a vital component in the delivery system as you ply your knowledge and skills. Consider it a tool as though you were starting out to build an edifice. A skilled

161

mechanic would not tear into a car without the proper wrenches. A competent artist would not start a painting without the proper brushes, canvas, paints. A cabinet maker chooses his tools carefully to insure the quality of his work.

A delivery system without enthusiasm is like a piano that is out of tune; the dullness and sour notes stand out and disharmony comes through. It is like an auto engine in need of tuning; choking and sputtering will not generate harmonious power. But tune the piano or tune the engine and enjoyable sounds of harmony strike the ears with satisfaction and good feelings.

Enthusiasm is an emotional reaction to the events of life. It is like happiness. Both are winning ingredients in an effective delivery method, that is, the manner you choose to offer your talents and abilities. Therefore, visualize at the outset that it is something over which you have complete control.

In the chapter sections that follow I will describe how you can develop or add more enthusiasm to your storehouse of tools. You will appreciate more and more the significant role that it plays in goal-setting, decision-making and people relations. It will enable you to absorb many new challenges and opportunities with increasing confidence.

Get Excited About Life

Does attitude toward your goals reflect excitement?

I anticipate that you are excited about the goals you are now pursuing. Am I correct? If your answer is yes, then I know you are on a positive thought track doing the things you enjoy whether at work or play. If your answer is no, then you are probably pursuing goals suggested by others or may have a fear of failing in your endeavor. Or perhaps your employer may have assigned some meaningless tasks. The work is drudgery and you just don't feel very productive. You are overcome by a defeatist attitude and can easily fabricate a number of mental excuses for failure such as:

"I can't be successful in the field."
"The work is degrading."
"My boss does not like me."

Failure is not defeat. It simply means you must implement some changes to be a success. It does not mean things are a complete loss. It does mean you have learned from experience. Enthusiasm, a positive emotion, has been deliberately blocked by negative thoughts. The defeatist attitude will continue until you drop the negativism and get on a positive track or change courses to satisfy your personal goals and self-esteem.

Gary Williams, a top science-oriented student, entered college to pursue an undergraduate degree in engineering. The curriculum was suggested by his parents and counselors. During the first year of general course study, Gary's name appeared regularly on the Dean's honor roll. Upon entering into engineering courses in the second year, Gary became discouraged, grades dropped, and he ultimately quit school. When asked why he responded, "I don't like school. I just want to find a job and go to work." As questions continued, he finally said, "I want to do my thing in life; I don't want to be an engineer." Then he said, "I only took the course to satisfy my parents—I hate to disappoint them. But that's the way it is."

Gary's goals had been set by others. He did not want to fail, but felt it was better to drop out than continue studying in a field that did not seem to satisfy his inner desires. Then while pondering his own future, Gary took a minor job as a learner-helper in the computer department of a large firm. He became mentally excited about studying and learning more in the computer field. Gary set new goals. This time they were his own. He returned to college to major in Computer Science. His academic achievements ranked him No. 1 in the class. Before completing the undergraduate work Gary set higher goals to pursue upon graduation—to obtain a master's degree in business. He achieved success in college and continued his growth career in business, rising to a top management position in just a few years.

Mental excitement is a powerful force. It is like a catalyst that when combined with other elements yields unbelievable strength. The key elements that put Gary Williams back on track were:

1. INCENTIVE OR DESIRE. Accomplishment must be preceded by a purpose, otherwise there is little need for enthusiasm. When a purpose exists that will enhance one's role in life, it's time to get excited.
2. WINNING ATTITUDE. Success is engendered by a positive thought process, an attitude to fulfill desires through diligent effort and application. Adopt a winning attitude in life and turn the revolving door of opportunity.
3. SPECIFIC GOALS. When the purpose is clear specific goals are easily prepared and the roadway to achievement paved with excitement. There is renewed enthusiasm at each mile post throughout the journey.
4. ACTION PLAN. When the goals are set, the steps to guide efforts to satisfactory completion fall in place—detours are avoided—the road map offers a clear route.
5. SELF-ESTEEM. A growth-oriented career in any role, academic or job related, continuously adds needed good thoughts about one's ability. Excitement to achieve builds with each step.
6. HAPPINESS. The satisfaction of reaching one level of accomplishment then moving forward to a higher level is an insatiable desire of the mentally excited achiever. Happiness and enthusiasm become vital tools for continued growth.

Examine your attitude toward the potential you have to offer, the vast opportunity to apply your talents and abilities for a greater share of life's riches. Discover that enthusiasm is within you. It may be dormant. You can light the catalyst of enthusiasm by adopting a worthwhile incentive or desire, a winning attitude, and specific goals. The excitement of life awaits your acceptance.

Delivery enthusiasm is a visible trait of the achiever.

Illuminate with Action

Do your actions send out rays of enthusiasm?

"When someone lights a lamp, does he put a box over it to shut out the light? Of course not! The light couldn't be seen or used. A lamp is placed on a stand to shine and be useful." These words recorded in the gospel of Mark many years ago are relevant today and every day as they reveal, among other things, the power of the spirit of enthusiasm. Why hide a good thing? Bring it out in the open for all to see and let the light illuminate your pathway to achievement.

Acts that reflect enthusiasm are like a light; they cast an unmistakable emotion of excitement. William James, a Harvard psychologist, said, "A person feels the way he acts." Feelings stem from emotions. Thus it becomes apparent that you must have something to feel good about before you can act enthusiastically. Right!

The interests you have in life are the basis for bright or dull sparks of enthusiasm. Interests stem from knowledge and experience. Obviously as your base of knowledge and experience is expanded, the greater the foundation of interest. You become interested in those things of which you have the greatest knowledge. And the more you know the more you want to know. It becomes an endless cycle of knowledge building on interest.

What can you do to bring your interests and knowledge into the open? How can you illuminate with action? Some time ago I coined the word WATTSEEDO, pronounced WATT—SEE—DO, each syllable being given equal weight. The word depicts your level of Visibility, the ability to Visualize, and the amount of your Vitality. These three V's can turn the spotlight on you and help you achieve still another "V" with enthusiasm, Victory. Consider the powers in each of these three ingredients:

1. VISIBILITY—Your WATT power. Is it 25 watts or less, perhaps 100, or even unlimited? The results of your efforts in any role are largely dependent on being out front and seen by others.

On a recent speaking engagement I shared the platform with two very interesting people. One was a talented young man seeking an opportunity to enhance his knowledge of communications. He was blind. The other was a successful businessman who shared his mastery of communication skills with an attentive audience. He was confined to a wheel-chair. Both bubbled with energy and enthusiasm. The entire audience watched their every move. The applause was loud and long.

Both men had learned to cope with their handicaps. They had gained enough WATT power and courage to move out front. Being visible gave them self-confidence, the vital ingredient for success in any endeavor.

2. VISUALIZE—Your SEE power. Do you see yourself as others see you or are the blinders cutting off your view? Choice of clothing, hair style, stance, facial expression, voice, grammar, and other personal characteristics cast an image of the total you for others to see. Personal goals, achievements, and acceptance are influenced by the way others see you.

We tend to cast an appearance and style that matches our interests and desires. For example, the contented ol' tramp looks the role because that is his life style. The actor dresses to portray a specific role and character. We, too, are acting out a chosen role. Some may prefer to just be stagehands and stay in the background. Others want to be out front where their performance can be seen and judged. By applying this two-way SEE power, your act can be changed to match the level of success you wish to achieve.

3. VITALITY—Your DO power. This implies portraying

an image that attracts attention, actions that reflect vigor, strength, enthusiasm. Ask yourself: "Am I the stagehand or the actor?" "For which role does my interest and knowledge qualify me?" Now examine your DO power.

"We are our actions, not our words," is a relevant maxim. The vital signs that will put you out front as a growing achiever are like the light placed in the open to shine and be useful. Turn on your WATT power as bright as knowledge and interest will allow. If it is too weak to achieve desired goals, then add knowledge and interest to expand the light. Apply SEE power to insure the total image is clear. Put DO power to work with constructive and well planned actions. Then your light will illuminate stepping stones ahead both for you and those who choose to join your newly discovered power of enthusiasm.

Delivery visibility, visualization, and vitality light the road to victory.

Spread Optimism

Do you approach challenges with optimistic thoughts?

Success in any endeavor implies a high degree of optimism and confidence plus a good feeling that the end results will serve a useful purpose for all concerned. Your state of mind thus becomes a very significant factor in achieving anything.

> Two men look out from prison bars,
> One saw mud, the other stars.

You can attune your thoughts to achieving either favorable or unfavorable results. Thoughts based on sound knowledge and experience is a far more realistic base for optimism and expectancy of a favorable outcome. Conversely, without a base for sound judgment optimism may give way to wishful thinking. Therefore, view optimism as a companion of confidence, an internal feeling based on a sense of realism.

Artisans devised the sundial to compete with the magic and mystery of time. That is why sundials carry a thought for remembrance with minutes that pass. An optimist's inscription read, "I record none but sunny hours." A realist inscription read, "It is later than you think." Optimism is a valued building tool when tempered with realism and based on solid facts. I encourage the adoption of this process as you build optimistic thoughts for yourself and others.

Many have failed believing that optimistic thoughts alone generate success. Like the fellow who waits for his ship to come in—when he hasn't sent one out. Or, the person who thinks when his shoes wear out he will be back on his feet.

The stage for optimism is set by things you think and do. Optimistic thoughts are the blossoms of seeds of cheerfulness, a smile, expectancy, courage, and confidence.

Cheerfulness ranks high among the virtues of optimism. It brings peace of mind which is, of course, good for your disposition and a healthy outlook. It gains the goodwill and friendship of others. Few think about the need to be cheerful at work. They seem to prefer frowns, perhaps to impress others with diligence and attention to duty—rather than results. But in social activities or at play cheerfulness is worn with ease and grace. Why not be as cheerful at work as at play? Try it.

Smiling is an expression of happiness, but also a strong reflection of a winning attitude. Losers are seldom seen wearing smiles, possibly shedding tears. Wearing a winning smile is an indication that you are credible, trustworthy, and responsive both as an individual and as a member of society. The frown takes on the appearance of a struggler, strained and drained with fear of failure.

Expectancy is the messenger of good news that things are going to turn out as anticipated. It combats worries, anxieties, and ill health. Petty problems fall by the wayside. Important matters that affect end results become priorities.

Courage is found in overall strength. It stems from developing and keeping in balance your four resources of power. These are, as you read in earlier chapters, your physical, mental, social, and spiritual resources.

Confidence is the spirit of assuredness flowing from the awareness that you are on the right road to achievement. It is a result of careful planning plus the development of accurate, detailed blueprints of the direction you propose to travel. When you know where you are headed and the route to take, there is no fear of getting lost or falling off the deep end. Results are in vision at the starting point.

Spreading optimism starts within you. It becomes a part of your actions when all resources have been cultivated and balanced. By adopting a cheerful, smiling, expectant, courageous, and confident approach to life's daily opportunities you automatically exude that same feeling to others. I encourage you to build your optimism on a base of realism. Avoid any phony, half-hearted reflections of whimsical thoughts. Spread truth, fairness, helpfulness, and confidence. Then others will join the circle to share your optimism and enthusiasm. A thought to ponder from an unknown author states:

> It is easy enough to be happy
> When life flows along like a song,
> But the man worthwhile
> Is the man with a smile
> When everything goes dead wrong.

Delivery optimism based on realism is worthy of spreading to others.

Reinforce Your Incentives

Do you possess the determination to achieve?
The ability to sustain a concentrated endeavor over an extended period may hit moments of weakness, if only fleet-

ing. There may be occasional temptation to yield to depression. However, the enthused are able to bolster their self-derived power over ever-increasing periods of time. They possess a strong determination to win. Setbacks may occur, but this provides time for reflection to overcome obstacles, to separate facts from opinions and move forward.

The achiever does not give up or blame others for setbacks. Instead he assumes the responsibility for his actions. He responds to the problems at hand, makes timely changes and decisions.

I have indicated heretofore that an incentive to accomplish anything must start with a worthwhile purpose. The most prudent planner recognizes that while an initial incentive may be adequate, reinforcement is required from time to time to keep the stimulus alive.

The project to put man on the moon underwent many design and mechanical modifications before successfully launching the flight. All developments—chemical, mechanical, and others—undergo frequent changes to achieve an acceptable product. Therefore, consider that all projects, small and large, individual and group-oriented may require change as they progress. Incentives need frequent and thoughtful reinforcement to keep the fire of potential burning. This necessitates amplifying incentives to sustain interest. Planned rewards should be highlighted often to keep them in prominent view for all concerned. Look upon incentives as the pedestal for interest and enthusiasm—they are a primary goal stimulus.

Charles Schwab was noted for his ability to build on incentives and arouse continued enthusiasm among employees. Perhaps this was a primary tool that contributed to his rapid rise from the storeroom to Chairman of Bethlehem Steel. He said, "The way to develop the best that is in a man is by appreciation and encouragement. I believe in giving a man an incentive to work. So I am anxious to praise, but loath to find fault."

Stimuli includes fear of punishment, loss of security, and

hope of reward. If corrective steps are not applied to foster good results, product quality and productivity decreases. If credit is withheld when good work is done, there is no incentive to put forth the best effort.

Love is considered the greatest constraining power of all. The person who loves his job, hobby, sport, and other activities needs no other incentive for action. But not everyone loves his role—hence the need to frequently reinforce incentives to attain results.

Personal and group projects should be treated in the same manner. That is, timely rewards should be set up at mile posts along the route even for yourself. It might be a night out, a day off, a movie, an addition to the wardrobe. Incentives are the stimuli that individuals or groups respond to and strive for.

The prizes of achievement require effort, toil, and sometimes strife, but rewards are worth fighting for.

Delivery zeal is sustained with timely recognition and rewards.

Kindle a Fire of Joy

Do you reflect the enjoyment of life?

The recipients of your services will be very responsive to a joyful heart. When sincere joy is exhibited or expressed in a timely manner the viewer is immediately infected with happy thoughts.

Enthusiasm and enjoyment are like a contagious disease or a forest fire. Both spread rapidly on contact with the carrier or spark. Strange isn't it—you cannot kindle a flame in the heart of another person until it is burning within yourself! The greatest joy of all is in lighting that flame and watching the results. It is somewhat like lighting a fireplace, watching burning wood and trying to keep the fire going. A joy of my children when they were small was a lighted fireplace on cold, snowy evenings. Wood was not always ideal for burning. The very hard and green type would be difficult to start and sometimes equally difficult to keep burning. On reflection, that experience resembles some type of people—cold, hard, and difficult to get started, and equally difficult to keep them going. In due time I traded the matches and newspapers used to light the fireplace for a gas jet. That took the delay and drudgery out of starting tough wood. The gas jet, on reflection, also reminds me of some people. Very responsive to a spark and easy to keep inflamed with the joys of life.

You have perhaps experienced these two types of people. The ineffective, responding only to direction and being driven; time is to be spent, not used. The effective types— I call them achievers. Their actions relate to the circumstance of events and attitudes of the people involved. They are conscious of timing. To paraphrase the book of Ecclesiastes, they know that for everything there is a season and a right time for every activity:

> A time to weep and a time to laugh,
> A time to mourn and a time to dance,
> A time to reject and a time to love,
> A time to be silent and a time to speak,
> A time for work and a time for play.

"Everything is appropriate in its own time—there is nothing better for a man to be happy and enjoy himself as long as he can and enjoy the fruits of his labor, for these are gifts from God."

The cultivation of joy in your life and its timely transfer to others is a vital thread of happiness and longevity. For every ounce of joy that you generate an immeasurable amount of hope is created. Joy is a feeling experienced today. Hope is the feeling of today's joy. It is the cherished spirit of life's fabric. "Of all the forces that make for a better world, none is so indispensable, none so powerful as hope.

Without hope men are only half alive. With hope they dream, think and work," reflected Charles Sawyer.

The power of hope or lack of it is often seen among the sick, aged, and lonesome. Where hope has faded, joy gives way to apathy, despair, and misery. Where it exists even the most destitute can smile and talk about a brighter tomorrow.

The power of enthusiasm in your delivery system will be gauged by the joy you create daily and the hope generated for tomorrow in those with whom you associate. Accept the challenge of igniting and nourishing joy, then watch your achievement quotient grow.

Delivery spirit is aglow where joy and hope abide.

A summary of key points in each chapter section and a listing of the apothegms are offered for your review and reference:

1. Nothing great was ever achieved without enthusiasm. It is a vital component in the delivery system. Enthusiasm is an emotion over which you have sole control.
2. The excitement about life is reflected in one's attitude toward work and play. Those who thoroughly enjoy and love the things they are doing need little else to motivate them toward greatness.
3. Put your lamp of enthusiasm where it can be seen and render a useful purpose. Enthusiasm stems from interests and knowledge. The more you know the more you want to know. Apply WATTSEEDO power and reach for victory.
4. Sound knowledge and experience is a realistic base for optimism. Don't mislead yourself or others with wishful thinking. Optimism is created by things you say and do.
5. Sustained enthusiasm requires frequent and thoughtful reinforcement of incentives. Set up appropriate rewards at mile posts along goal routes for yourself and others.
6. It is impossible to kindle a flame of joy in the heart of another until one is burning within yourself. Cultivate joy in your life and then transfer it to others at the appropriate time.

APOTHEGMS

1. *Delivery enthusiasm is a visible trait of the achiever.*
2. *Delivery visibility, visualization, and vitality light the road to victory.*
3. *Delivery optimism based on realism is worthy of spreading to others.*
4. *Delivery zeal is sustained with timely recognition and rewards.*
5. *Delivery spirit is aglow where joy and hope abide.*

11
Self-Esteem Power

> *You cannot teach a man anything.*
> *You can only help him discover it*
> *within himself.*
>
> —Galileo

(DELIVERY)

Do you have a high regard for yourself?

The most important value-judgment man can make is the one he makes about himself. The estimate of this value is not one that you might express in words. It comes in the form of an emotional response that is experienced in feelings about life, activities, events, circumstances. There is, in a sense, a constant value-response meter clicking away in your thought process rendering an appraisal of feelings. It moves up and down like a bank account registering deposits and crediting withdrawals.

Appraisal of what you think about yourself has a significant effect on your values and goals. In turn, your motivation level is influenced. Since the delivery system used in offering talents and abilities is a prime factor in acceptance by others, the power of self-esteem becomes a gigantic force. A low esteem may contribute to self-imposed weaknesses and lead to failure. A high esteem, as long as it is not falsely inflated, will support essential strengths for achievement.

The base of self-esteem is seated in two interrelated factors, self-confidence and self-respect. These were discussed in Chapter 1 as they relate to Compassion. They represent one's sense of competency toward a chosen role and a sense of personal worth. The need for self-esteem is inherent in man's nature. Self-worth and acceptance by others is a basic means of survival; too, the power of choosing is a free exercise of man's will.

Self-esteem is not a list of traits, talents, or abilities. Rather it is a feeling, often deep and sometimes rooted in the depths of childhood experiences, that give rise to positive and negative emotions and resultant life values.

Since the starting point of self-esteem is internal, it is appropriate to look within and consider those feelings that influence your goals and desires. It is often the unseen or underlying weaknesses that create obstacles to progress. These are a basis for improvement and potential growth.

Be Introspective

Are you mindful of your strengths and weaknesses?

Everyone has strengths, but also weaknesses. Most experience fears and occasional negative feelings about themselves. The fact that weaknesses and negativism exist at times is unimportant. The importance lies in what is done to overcome them. Some people tend to put up false fronts, cover up their mistakes, or run away from the problems. Weaknesses control their lives and they suffer from low self-esteem.

While recruiting technical and administrative personnel for a large company, I had an occasion to interview several candidates for the position of training manager. It is often difficult to find the desired match of academic exposure and experience. After interviewing many candidates the ideal match appeared. A man with excellent academic credentials from a mid-western university plus ideal industrial experience. It happened that I also had exposure at the same university as the candidate. When discussing buildings, sports, and campus environment, the candidate's answers were vague and questionable. A phone call to the registrar's office revealed the candidate had never attended the university. When confronted, he said, "I simply could not get good interviews for the position I wanted without identifying a college background." While falsifying academic credentials or buying certificates of graduation is not new, it does reveal human failings. A foundation built on false evidence is like a house built on sand. It will not stand the test of time. It leads to a fear complex and a low self-esteem.

On one of the first jobs in my working life, I was employed as an accounting clerk with a public accounting firm. I, together with several other employees, was responsible for verifying the accuracy of client audit reports. On one occasion I goofed badly and let a $100,000 error slip through on a report for a major company. The client discovered the error and called the company president. The accounting firm was put in a bad light. Their credibility had been jeopardized. Naturally the search was on to determine the error source. Our working copies carried initials of each clerk. But in this case, the initials were obscure. It was difficult to determine who allowed the error to get through, but I knew and chose to cover up. I froze in fear of "losing my job." Ultimately, my self-esteem reached a new low as a result of a guilty conscience. I became so depressed that my feelings seemed more important than the job. So I confessed to the president—the error was mine. He responded with stern words, "I thought it was you, but I decided to let you stew in your own juice. Now that you have confessed, let it be a lesson to you. You placed the company in a bad situation with a good client. Perform your work for others to admire, never for condemnation." The lesson was a lasting one. Sheltering mistakes, falsifying one's record of accomplishments create feelings of guilt, fear, inferiority complex. The resultant negative feelings lower self-esteem and impair performance as well as acceptance by others.

Introspection is a simple way to assess feelings; it is an easy way to identify strengths and weaknesses although many are unwilling to approach this step. Who better than you can look within and match feelings with desires and goals? Examination of one's own mental status and attitude toward the world of people and work requires deep thought. Honesty in self-study must prevail for a realistic analysis. Professional counseling should be a first consideration when deemed appropriate.

Delivery strength requires self-evaluation to maximize growth.

Evaluate Your Self-Esteem

Do you carry a picture of self-worth in your mind?
Much of the improvement made in upgrading talents and abilities is dependent on personal evaluation and effort. The driving force is usually a specific purpose to fulfill a burning desire. However, to improve anything one must know what constitutes improvement and how to achieve it. This, in turn, depends on a whole system of value-judgment.

Each person has developed his own set of values from life's experiences; he makes decisions and choices in keeping with such values accordingly. But unless these values harmonize with those who use your services, success becomes an uphill struggle. People simply pick those they want to do business with based on their own system of values. Therefore, to develop a preferred mental picture of self-worth, it is appropriate to evaluate your current degree of self-esteem. Then determine areas that merit logical improvement to match the values leading to the most effective delivery system for you.

For a starter, ask yourself: "Are there any emotional road blocks in my delivery system that prevent me from achieving my goals?" "What can I do to upgrade my value judgments in harmony with my goals and with those who will help me reach them?" Since self-esteem is a feeling about life and the circumstances surrounding it your self-evaluation should point to those many situations that influence feelings. For example: Do you feel superior or inferior? Are you an introvert, extrovert, or ambivert? Are you a warm, friendly personality or a cold loner? Is your attitude positive or negative? Do you cover up mistakes, render false reports, blame others? Are you offensive or defensive? Are you cooperative? Are you compulsive, complacent, open-minded, confident? Are you a perfectionist?

I have indicated heretofore that 95 percent of people problems are self-imposed—these arise from our own system of value judgments. Only about 5 percent of human problems are a result of external influences. Hence, evaluation of self-esteem is very much an inward look.

There is no hard and fast set of rules that I would boldly portray for you to mold the ideal self-esteem or system of values. Everyone is different and unique in his heritage, awareness, and experience. Introspection, self-evaluation, and professional counseling are appropriate avenues. However, Reverend Henry Van Dyke did set forth four significant rules that I believe are of great value. These should not be viewed as conclusive, but will surely be helpful.

> Four things a man must learn to do
> If he would keep his record true;
> To think without confusion clearly;
> To love his fellowman sincerely;
> To act from honest motives purely;
> To trust in God and heaven securely.

Delivery harmony with associates builds solid relationships.

Increase Your Awareness

Are you continuously expanding your total awareness?

Awareness is a very comprehensive term. As defined by Lilburn S. Barksdale, "It incorporates many factors, including everything we perceive with our five senses as well as everything we perceive instinctively, and intuitively, both consciously and non-consciously. It is the product of the total conditioning of our entire life experience, plus our innate intelligence and intuition. It is responsible for our insights, inner urges, emotional reactions, and every decision we make." (P. 12, *Building Self-Esteem,* by Lilburn S. Barksdale copyright 1972.)

Personal growth results from increased total awareness. Every link of progress represents a value level to the achiever and a stepping stone to even higher values. The desire to grow is inherent in most people since life is growth by nature. A healthy self-esteem, that is, to feel good about one's self, is paramount to growth.

The failure to increase total awareness leads to incompetence and low self-esteem. Dr. Lawrence J. Peter and Raymond Hull, authors of *The Peter Principle* (copyright 1969, published by William Morrow and Company, Inc.) suggested, "In a hierarchy every employee tends to rise to his level of incompetence—work is accomplished by those employees who have not yet reached their level of incompetence." This satirical writing about man's tendency to escalate himself to oblivion at his level of incompetence magnifies what happens when one fails to keep abreast, to grow, to continuously upgrade total awareness.

The rapidly changing environment of technology, economics, and social customs necessitate on-going study for growth and progress. Self-esteem or feelings are at stake. The winner will push on and achieve. Losers will fall by the wayside in highly competitive situations. Therefore, it is important to know where one stands, what is expected. Such awareness is a reinforcer of good self-esteem.

Written appraisals of employee performance are used extensively in business and industry. Usually appraisal forms are completed annually by managers on their subordinates. However, some managers ask the employee to complete his own appraisal following a specific format. Then the manager and subordinate discuss their mutual assessment.

Appraisal forms usually call for a listing of objectives and a rating of results on each. Too, performance characteristics such as attitude, initiative, and relationships are included and require written comments. This technique has much merit as it forces the employee to be introspective. In my experience, 95 percent of the employees writing their own appraisals were more critical and constructive of their performance than were their managers. It indicates that, in most instances, people will realistically assess their efforts and future needs.

Total awareness of performance and suggestions to expand your potential will stimulate self-esteem. Consider the following listing of typical characteristics that influence work performance, also the acceptance by others:

Attitude	Creativity	Output Quality
Knowledge	Enthusiasm	Output Quantity
Skills	Dependability	Organizing Ability
Initiative	Relationships	Self-Confidence
Judgment	Job Interest	Self-Control

Relate each word to your daily activities and goals. Add your own choice of words as they come to mind. Be introspective; then rate yourself on each factor using a scale of 1–5.

If you discover areas that need development to enhance the delivery system for your talents and abilities, then adopt plans for action. You will be increasing your total awareness with each self-development effort. Achievement will be a consequence of a healthy self-esteem—a good feeling about yourself will propel you to new heights.

Delivery techniques improve as awareness grows.

Feel Good About Yourself

Do you generate good feelings about yourself?
The ultimate need of all people is to feel good about themselves. Most humans harbor an innate desire to feel important and feel a sense of self-worth. While some jobs

181

may not provide total satisfaction, many seek other activities such as hobbies, sports, community roles to fill the void. The desire for happiness, peace of mind, and performing worthwhile endeavors is a driving force.

Everyone has probably met a negative person—the type who enjoys spreading gloom. Or the type who is forever complaining about their aches and pains—it seems they just enjoy the worst of health. Their underlying happiness stems from the attention and recognition received through constant negativism. A humorous experience occurred to Mrs. Evelyn Jones, a perpetual complainer about her health problems. On one occasion she complained that the pains in her legs were so bad that she became bedfast, simply unable to walk. Her husband, Alex, did his best to provide care until they finally arranged for their doctor to make a house visit. The doctor carried out a thorough examination and suggested they might want to place her in a hospital for further tests. He then took the husband by the arm, moved away from the sick bed, and began whispering to Alex, saying, "I don't think there is anything very much wrong with Evelyn." Then in a loud voice he said, "Let me just leave a prescription here on the dresser—get it filled and we will see if that helps." He took Alex by the arm and left the room. When they had gone, Evelyn got out of bed, walked to the dresser and read the prescription. It said, "Now that you are out of bed, keep on walking and enjoy life."

Feeling good about yourself, your work, and other activities is paramount to having an effective delivery system. If the circumstance that surrounds your interests do not engender such a spirit then you should take a serious look at the circumstances. In virtually all instances, you will discover that the circumstances are of your own making, thus changes will often be things you can accomplish and overcome.

Two sources of the greatest potential for contentment are satisfying work and love. Worthwhile work gives man an opportunity to apply his knowledge, skill, and experience. It provides an opportunity to experience a sensitivity of self-worth and importance. The bond of love fulfills a vital psychological need for human companionship with whom he can share and enjoy life.

People who have attained a measure of success often say that the period of greatest satisfaction and high esteem was during the pursuit of goals. The internal chemistry that takes place when desire, opportunity, and challenge are combined with talent and ability creates a zest for life. The desire for human companionship affords man the interest and pleasure of dealing with people on a business and social basis. They develop feelings of love and affection for others that satisfy their belonging needs in life.

Many things generate good feelings and millions of people constantly seek out the ones that provide them satisfaction. Often people do not seem to know what will fulfill their pleasure needs, yet search and try an endless array of pursuits without success.

Counseling and consulting experiences have afforded me an opportunity to study human behavior extensively and assess several major areas that evoke good feelings. Eight such circumstances are discussed and hopefully will serve as a stimulus for you:

1. POSSESSIONS USED. People accumulate many tangible possessions for use in their homes, offices, and elsewhere. Some are for convenience, some for comfort, and usually a portion is just for show. The books, clothes, tools, toys, sports equipment, and all other items in frequent use provide maximum satisfaction. A vivid example is the child with a vast choice of expensive toys who prefers an empty spool on a string or a tattered doll. Look first for joy in the things you use.

2. CHOICES MADE. The eyes are bigger than the stomach, so we learned as a child. Our tastes in clothes, cars, and houses are often more costly than we can afford. Emotional reactions guide many decisions. But

it is usually the well thought out careful choices that provide the most satisfaction. I am guilty of irrational decisions as are most people. Perhaps you too have purchased things you could have survived without and been better off economically. Exercising our greatest power—that of choice, offers much satisfaction, but sometimes disappointment.

3. PRIORITIES PURSUED. Imagination tends to lead the most competent people astray. When priorities are thoughtfully evaluated, ranked according to potential worth, and then pursued, the anticipation and effort to reach a predetermined result provides the most satisfaction. It is the projects in hand that offer potential happy results, not wishful thinking that absorbs productive time.

4. COMPASSION PUT FORTH. The opportunity to share interests, cultivate favorable relationships, build friendships, love and be loved, are the basis for happiness in life. But much is dependent on one's own efforts. The bridge to happiness awaits the compassionate.

5. TRUTHS CONVEYED. The person who speaks the truth walks with confidence. The prevaricator or the one who thrives on fabricated stories needs an exceptional memory to avoid pitfalls—he walks in fear that someone will discover his faults. Sincerity, the naked truth, and loyalty generate satisfaction.

6. RESULTS OBTAINED. There is little doubt that good results are a builder of great feelings. The success of free enterprize is a glistening example of results emanating from happy workers. The results-oriented person is on a success track.

7. GIFTS TO OTHERS. A matchless feeling comes over a person when others accept their gifts. A gift or reward is a consequence of a relationship or service—nothing stimulates good feelings like recognition.

8. THE WAY YOU LIVE. The standards you follow, values you set, integrity portrayed, feelings generated in

others about what you are, is a picture to behold. It can represent a source of much satisfaction or distress to you and the lives you touch. In turn, it offers highest dividends of self-worth or degradation—the way you live speaks for itself.

The greatest builder of satisfaction and self-esteem in life is within. You are the creator of circumstances that unfold the warmth of self-worth in yourself and that which you share. Make a winning delivery system your goal. Then feel good about life and enjoy the rewards of feeling good about yourself.

Delivery satisfaction is a result of satisfying others.

Take Charge of Your Life

Are you enjoying a satisfying and fulfilling life?
The person who is enjoying life to the fullest will be maintaining a high self-esteem. He will be experiencing a happy, healthy, and productive life. Too, he will be very much in charge of the factors that are contributing to a satisfying and fulfilling life. If you are not experiencing a similar role something is amiss, your self-esteem will not be what it could be. Your delivery system is at stake and will not be producing its potential.

The person in charge of a plane or ship usually carries the title of captain. The subordinate members are known by various titles; collectively they comprise the crew. The captain carries great responsibility for insuring his ship is in proper order, that all essential resources for a successful journey are aboard, and that the trip is well planned. Your role in life can be equated to that of the ship's captain who has authority and responsibility for decisions and choices. Or, it can be equated to that of a crew member who carries out the orders of others. While the jobs of the captain and crew are all important, the primary difference is that only one makes the final decisions and choices while others follow directions.

The power of your self-esteem is dependent on the freedom to make decisions about yourself, to make choices, to think, act, and do. Freedom, of course, carries with it the responsibility for such actions. You must be willing to pay the price demanded of freedom. Many roles at varying organization levels offer freedom to act within policies and guidelines. There are numerous jobs, particularly those controlled by machines and automation, that limit the freedom to think—routines are already defined. While many find satisfaction in routine jobs and menial tasks, the greatest opportunity to build high self-esteem occurs where freedom with responsibility exists.

Accept the reality that you are your own authority; that you do have an innate desire to fulfill your potential; that you have the freedom in this free country to pick and choose; that you are responsible for your attitude toward all things, your reactions and choices. Therein lies high or low self-esteem.

You are indeed a unique human being and within you is the power to grow in awareness and love. The horizons are as bright and as close as you paint and perceive them. Failure to fulfill your ambitions will be a momentary obstacle for reflection if you will recognize:

1. You cannot accomplish more than your total awareness permits. To do more requires that you know more and are able to do more.
2. Growth is limited to the extent that your four resources have been developed and maintained to the maximum of your ability, that is, physical, mental, social, spiritual resources.
4. Positive thoughts of health, happiness, contentment, love, and growth are building blocks for high self-esteem. Negative thoughts that inflict physical or mental rejection—shame, remorse, guilt, hate, indifference,

self-pity, and all related innuendoes lead to low self-esteem. They crumble life's power potential like the ocean tides wash away yesterday's child-built sand castles.

5. The freedom to think, act, and do with responsibility gives you the power to take charge of your life and be your own authority.

Proverbs 17:27 says, "A cheerful heart does good like medicine, but a broken spirit makes one sick." These words reflect an image of a person in charge of his life versus one hampered by irresponsibility, uncontrolled thoughts that have allowed irrational decisions and poor choices to serve as guides.

When President Franklin D. Roosevelt died the world was at war. He had been responsible for many difficult and trying decisions. Upon learning of his death, Vice-President Harry Truman is reported to have said, "Oh my, what do we do now?" An aid responded, "Sir, you are now in charge." While it must have taken some time to collect his thoughts President Truman did indeed take charge. The annals of history reflect many great accomplishments in his presidential years.

You too can take charge of events in your life and utilize self-esteem power to make your delivery system produce a "cheerful heart that does good like medicine."

Delivery freedom, with responsibility, shapes high self-esteem.

A review of the chapter sections and apothegms on the importance of self-esteem in the delivery of your wares will remind you of pertinent thoughts:

1. The most important value-judgment man can make is the one he makes about himself. Mere words will not define this value—it is an emotional response that you experience in feelings about life.

2. Strengths and weaknesses abound in everyone. Introspection

is a simple method of assessing feelings, attributes, areas of need. Who better than you can look within.

3. Each person uses a self-developed value system; it serves him in making decisions and choices. Harmony of relationship with others is dependent on compatible standards.
4. Personal growth results from increased total awareness. Failure to increase awareness leads to incompetence and resultant low self-esteem.
5. The ultimate need of all people is to feel good about themselves. It is essential to feel good about life, work, and other activities, to have an effective delivery system.
6. Self-esteem power is dependent on the freedom to make decisions about yourself. Accept the reality that you have that freedom, with responsibility, to think, act, and do.

APOTHEGMS

1. *Delivery strength requires self-evaluation to maximize growth.*
2. *Delivery harmony with associates builds solid relationships.*
3. *Delivery techniques improve as awareness grows.*
4. *Delivery satisfaction is a result of satisfying others.*
5. *Delivery freedom, with responsibility, shapes high self-esteem.*

12
Self-Confidence Power

The rung of a ladder was never meant to rest upon, but only to hold a man's foot long enough to enable him to place the other one higher.

—Thomas Huxley

(DELIVERY)

Are accomplishments a habit with you?

Philosophers throughout the ages have pinpointed confidence as a primary component of success. Everyone who has been successful in business, politics, sports, stage, or screen, will identify confidence as the force that propelled them to achievement.

Proponents of achievement patterns, including myself, hold self-confidence as a key to personal growth. The reason is simple. You cannot accomplish anything significant without first thinking you can. The basis for confident thinking is rooted in habits. Thus, self-confidence comes from the habit of accomplishment. Like so many realities in life the sequence of "thought—accomplishment—confidence, thought—accomplishment—confidence" becomes an end-

189

less cycle for those who think. Of course keeping your self-confidence at a high peak is not always easy. There are many external influences and emotional reactions in every situation. These sources of thoughts and feelings tend to clutter the mind, and doubt occurs. Unsureness results from the myriad of new thoughts. Setbacks and defeats will occur. But failure does not ruin the career of the courageous. Failure represents nothing more than a red stoplight that compels one to stop, think, react with cautious judgment, and move forward on the green light.

There is an excellent way to maintain the momentum of accomplishment in the face of occasional setbacks. Simply hold tightly in your mind the thought that new learning is being acquired from the experience and it will lead you to greater heights. "Search for the seeds of victory in every disaster and the seeds of disaster in every victory," advised Napoleon Hill.

When you have given the best that is within you and lost, be proud of your accomplishment and use the experience as a building block. John Wooden, famed UCLA head basketball coach placed his ideals of personal and athletic achievement in a hierarchy that he calls "The Pyramid of Success." The elements of his pyramid are the building blocks of character. The cornerstones are industriousness and enthusiasm. The summit is competitive greatness, supported by poise and confidence. John says he never mentioned winning in locker room talks. He says, "My last words before going out onto the court were: 'When this game is over, I want your heads up—and the only way for them to be up is for you to play the best you possibly can. If you do that, the score will probably be to your liking. And if it isn't, that means the other team was better. There's nothing wrong with that.' "

The lengthy championship boxing career of Mohammed Ali is often heralded as one of the greatest of all time. His successful three-time reign and occasional defeat were highlighted by his frequent comment, "I am the greatest." His career indicates he sincerely believed that statement—it became a trademark. It may occasionally have influenced overconfidence which can be destructive; such feelings lead to arrogance—an attitude that few will tolerate.

The focus in this chapter is on helping you develop and use self-confidence power to build a winning attitude, an effective delivery system. Be conscious of reality as we proceed—underconfidence prevents success; confidence is built on the habit of accomplishments; repeated successes sometimes lead to overconfidence; a cock-sure attitude stimulates arrogance and leads to defeat.

Believe in Yourself

Do you believe in your ability?

Belief is a powerful force. What you believe affects your life more than any single factor. A change in belief will change your actions and feelings.

A group of young campers were backpacking in a West Virginia woods. Stopping at a spring, they filled their water canteens and drank. Three strangers came upon the group and, intending to have a little fun, explained that the water was known to be contaminated; they said it had made other campers deathly ill. The strangers soon realized their joke was having unexpected results. Several in the party became very ill and it took much effort to get the sick out of the woods for treatment. What happened? Was the water really polluted? No, the water was quite safe to drink. But the powerful force of belief soured the digestive process of those who became ill.

Out of beliefs goals are achieved. Out of achievement habits are formed. Out of habits confidence is built. Confidence in ability shapes destination.

It becomes apparent that belief in one's self and ability to be successful is the basis for accomplishment. Results don't just happen, you must make them happen, and the starting point, as in all of life's activities, is with thought.

The behavior of every person reveals two distinct personality types. Thought patterns identify the type you reflect. For example, when thoughts of fear, doubt, anxiety enter the mind—as in the case of the campers—negative feelings control your reactions. Emotions will cause you to act without confidence, to walk hesitatingly, become ill, move out of the front line of activity and await guidance or leadership from others. But when positive thoughts of personal achievement, awareness of knowledge, skill, health, and physical strength enter your mind, a conscious effort will be made to take the lead—confidence exudes and you move forward.

There is an old maxim that says, "Success comes in cans, not in cannots." Accomplishment obviously stems from positive thoughts of "I can." Negative thoughts of "I cannot" lead to self-defeat. Eliminate them from your vocabulary and unlock your mind to receive thoughts that lead to accomplishment.

How can you unlock this door to your confidence potential? It's all in your thought process, so unlock the door to this storeroom and walk through. There's an ancient story of a king who used a special test to help him choose between three equally qualified candidates for prime minister. He arranged for the best locksmiths to devise a very complex lock which was placed on a palace door. Then he brought the three men into the room and said, "The prime minister will be the one who can open the door." Two of the men reacted emotionally to the challenge; fear of failure flashed through their minds. Both started making mathematical calculations in hopes of determining the combination of the lock. The third man believed he could open the door. He stared intently at the lock, then confidently walked to the door, turned the knob, and the door opened. It had never been locked.

You too can unlock your thought process of belief in yourself. God did not devise a secret combination for a lock to secure this reservoir of confidence power. The only requirement is that you open the door. Here are five key factors that I believe will guide you in opening wide this channel of belief:

1. *Think positive thoughts*—all achievement, all riches, begin in the mind. You were given the greatest power of all, as indicated in Chapter 2, that of choice. Your mental attitude toward health, happiness, work, love, and life's many blessings is the source of bountiful riches. Think and act from positive thoughts.

2. *Acquire know-how*—before achievement can possibly occur one must possess the fundamental knowledge and skill to produce results. Expect to pay the price of obtaining whatever academic or other exposure it takes to do the things you want to do. Plan and work toward being the best at your vocation and avocation if you expect to lead the pack.

3. *Practice know-how*—invariably the skillful have converted knowledge to mental and physical actions through endless repetitive thoughts or motions. When a professional football player catches a 50-yard pass on the run and scores a touchdown, he is following a routine that he has doubtless practiced thousands of times. Accomplished musicians will have practiced a musical score over and over until they sense perfection and, in turn, confidence. People find contentment in a job only after routines are understood—this is a result of practicing know-how. It may be called force of habit, spaced repetition—the meaning is the same, that is, practice over and over to achieve perfection and the blossom of confidence will come forth.

4. *Seek harmony*—it is essential to harmonize your thoughts, actions, and motives with your conscience. You may find yourself striving to fulfill motives of others and not satisfying your inner self. Internal disharmony is destructive; it will prevent you from maximizing your potential. In addition to achieving internal harmony, you must seek external harmony with those who

share your circle of activities. Self-confidence, in the final analysis, results from belief in yourself—hence the value of internal harmony. The belief others have in you is a reflection of this confidence and support, thus the value of external harmony.

5. *Build with hope*—the barometer of happiness rises and falls with self-confidence. Hope is like a drop of mercury in a meter that moves up and down in a measuring tube when influenced by surrounding elements. Pursuing a worthy purpose or goal in harmony with one's total environment stimulates hope of accomplishment. "The great essentials of happiness are something to do, something to love, and something to hope for," suggested Alexander Chalmers.

Re-examine the five key factors and appreciate that the road to accomplishment is built on a deep foundation of thought. Your beliefs form the road's surface on which you travel. The journey will be as smooth or as rough as the power of belief in yourself. Apply these factors in your daily life; adopt an "I can" philosophy and feel your confidence grow.

Delivery belief in ability assures accomplishment.

Walk Tall

Does your posture reflect courage?

Many people can relate one or more incidents that have had a tremendous impact on their mental outlook and approach to life's challenges. I often wonder what my posture and confidence might have been today had I not responded to the wisdom of an elementary schoolteacher, Sadie Handy, who taught me to walk tall and think tall. She would say, "If you want to feel proud all over, you must walk tall and think tall."

It was an era in my young life when, for some reason I

can't recall today, I was experiencing learning doldrums. School was not exciting for me. My grades were passing, but would certainly not win any honors. One day Sadie said, "I have been observing your posture. Tell me, why are you walking all slouched over in the shoulders? You walk with a stoop that does not become you. And another thing. When you walk you seem to drag your heels and click the floor every step. Sounds like you do not have the strength to pick up your feet. Don't you feel good?" "Well, I thought I did," I replied. "If you feel good why don't you get your eyes off the floor, watch where you are going, and look at the beauty of the world instead of the floor?" Sadie spoke with a stern voice and usually when she spoke I had the good sense to listen, because she was usually right.

Sadie took my arm and stood me against the wall and said, "Now straighten up and make your entire body feel that wall; your shoulders, back, buttocks, heels. Hold your head high, pull in your chin and your stomach." I did as she advised. "Well, you do look better now," she said, "How do you feel?" I was a bit frightened, but responded, "OK, I guess." "Now I want you to walk in that posture back and forth across the room as tall as you can. Walk tall, that keeps your posture straight. Think tall, that keeps your head high, and keep doing it until you feel proud all over." Every few minutes she would say, "Walk tall, think tall and feel proud all over."

As I walked slowly across the room Sadie said "faster, pick up the tempo." She began to beat a rhythm on her desk like a drum and sing out a chant I shall never forget. "Walk tall, think tall, feel good all over." She repeated these words over and over. They became so etched in my mind that I can, to this day, visualize that event as though it happened yesterday. Too, I can still hear that drum beat and chant "Walk tall, think tall, feel good all over."

The habit of walking tall and thinking tall soon became natural. My mind became filled with personal pride about my posture even though it may not have been perfect. My interest and role in school activities increased as did my grades. From that day to this, I cherish the impact on my life of that simple message "Walk tall, think tall, feel good all over." I attribute much of my self-confidence, courage, and accomplishments to the memorable wisdom of these words.

It is no secret that body strength, energy, coordination, and balance are rooted in an erect stance. People are influenced to follow and model themselves after the one who reflects confidence and courage in his walk and other body actions. Few, if any, will choose to follow the weakling or a person lacking in courage.

In one of his war-time speeches, Winston Churchill admonished his countrymen and allies to be courageous. "Courage," he said, "is rightly esteemed the first of human qualities because it is the quality that guarantees all others." James Allen writing about courage said, "Whether you be man or woman you will never do anything in this world without courage. It is the greatest quality of the mind next to honor." About the significance of courage there can be no doubt, but it remains a missing attribute for many.

Author, speaker, and friend Cavett Robert shared "Three Bridges to Success" which had been very meaningful to him. I too found deep significance in visualizing bridges that span fear, build confidence, and lead on to greater heights. The three bridges are:

- Fear to Courage
- Courage to Confidence
- Confidence to Success

Visualize that each of the three statements form archlike bridges over a flowing stream and that each bridge has a name. The first bridge is called "Knowledge"; the second is called "Practice"; the third "Spaced Repetition." As you acquire knowledge and consciously practice and practice it at timely intervals, courage will overcome fear and lead you to pursue life confidently. With confidence secured in your mind, you can conquer unlimited horizons with ease.

Walk tall and think tall as you cross the three bridges to success. Then feel proud all over about the height of your self-confidence.

Delivery courage signifies confidence in end results.

Set Higher Standards

Do you set personal standards of excellence?

People possess real or imaginary standards in everything they do. In educational level, housing, job environment, physical attributes, social roles, yes, even in spiritual activities. Self-confidence to achieve follows the level of one's personal standards and remains at that level until the standards are raised.

Personal standards are the model you use as a comparison in measuring or judging adequacy. They represent your yardstick of values, become your precepts of commandments of action and conduct, touchstone, and level of excellence.

For example, if one's standard of adequate educational level is high school, then self-confidence to seek roles which require higher educational levels will be lacking. Heredity, coupled with knowledge, skills, and exposure that evolve through work experience will influence your confidence level and, in turn, the desire for higher standards—a better home, better car, luxuries. But this approach to achievement is one that tends to evolve with time rather than as a result of specific goals and action plans. In other words, things just happen, they were not preplanned.

Each honest endeavor, each walk of life, has its recognized leaders based on excellence of performance. Such front runners become examples or models which every aspiring challenger seeks to surpass. Olympic records in virtually every sport are set at each meet. The newly established marks become a new standard or target for future Olympians.

197

You may be saying to yourself "I am satisfied with what I have—why should I concern myself with standards?" Life does not stand still. Where there is no progress there is disintegration. Growth is change and decay. Therefore, failure to reach out, to keep abreast or seek new horizons in your field, explore or expand to new areas of interest is simply drifting in the boat of complacency. You are headed for stagnation and decay.

Few people will deliberately choose a course of stagnation. The excitement of daily events such as world news, TV entertainment, new innovations, new styles, space travel, spark the imagination to stay involved to some degree. But many do little to uplift their standards. They become victims of standards set by others, they are creatures of circumstances. Life is existence, not excitement and challenge.

Building a model of excellence is not an easy task. But there is no excellence without difficulty. Longfellow wrote "The supreme excellence is simplicity." The initial step is learning what is first rate and then pursuing it, not only in the job or activity which produces a living, but in all the great fields of life and, above all, in living itself. The second step is setting personal standards that, when achieved, will place you as high on the ladder of life as your overall competence allows. It is doing the best that you know how to do. Anyone can reach a level of mediocrity, many will reach the commonplace rank of average, few will achieve supreme excellence—unless of course they set higher standards.

Longfellow's approach to excellence is profound—let simplicity be your guide. The basis for setting higher standards is in structuring your goals so as to reach desired levels. Achieving the standards is dependent upon the action taken to meet and fulfill your goals. The likelihood of success is greatest when the goals are supported with an action plan as discussed in Chapter 3. Keep your goals simple in design, your action plan simple in application, but definitive in concept. Then achieving higher standards of excellence will be an enjoyable challenge even though they may be difficult.

Another basis for setting standards is adopting a personal

creed, a simple statement of your beliefs and aspirations. Chapter 4—"Control Input and Output" outlines the benefits of having a creed. When adopted, committed to memory, and applied daily it will serve as an inspiration to strive for higher standards, to put forth the best that is within you.

Four steps are commonly applied in business and industry to control and insure goal/action plan results are achieved. These are:

1. *Developing standards*—these become the criteria by which output and results are measured.
2. *Measuring performance*—recorded output serves to identify the work done.
3. *Evaluating performance*—work is analyzed to assess the quality and results attained.
4. *Correcting performance*—necessary changes or improvements are adopted to insure desired results will be achieved.

Simplicity is divine. The four steps of control are indeed simple and can readily be applied in setting and achieving your higher standards. Of course, the onus of action is in your hands. Let common sense, self-confidence, and faith be your guide in setting and reaching higher standards in life. Wishing will not make it so. Former President Calvin Coolidge said "Doubters do not achieve; skeptics do not contribute, cynics do not create. Faith is the great motive power, and no man realizes his full possibilities unless he has the deep conviction that life is eternally important, and that his work, well done, is part of an unending plan."

> Sitting still and wishing
> Made no person great
> The good Lord sends the fishing
> But you must dig the bait.

Delivery standards are a gauge of excellence.

Make Accurate Decisions

Is your decision batting average satisfactory?

Those who play in major league baseball stay in the game as long as their batting or pitching average is satisfactory. When slumps occur, and this happens to the best talent from time to time, then coaching and counseling is given to correct faults and restore confidence. Poor performers may be moved back to minor leagues for further development or dropped from the team.

The world of work and pleasure is performed on a similar field. All daily activities present a constant barrage of choices and, in turn, the necessity of deciding between your perception of right and wrong, good and bad, to do or not to do, buy now or later, pay cash or charge, and on and on. Accurate decisions can propel you into the big leagues; inaccurate ones can put you back in the minors or even be fatal.

The key ingredient in building and reflecting self-confidence is the habit of accomplishment—getting hits and homeruns, being a winning pitcher. It follows then as clearly as night follows day that accomplishment is a result of making accurate decisions, good choices.

Human failings notwithstanding, one's batting average will never reach and remain at a level of perfection. A sixth-century philosopher, Croesus, may have had similar thoughts when he said: "There is a wheel on which the affairs of men revolve, and its mechanism is such that it prevents any man from always being fortunate."

Failures will occasionally occur in any human endeavor. Some decisions are quick, spur of the moment choices based on scant information, personal biases, and emotional reactions. But the fewer the failures the better. It is not merely a case of win some, lose some. Rather it is a case of good judgment versus poor judgment.

The accurate decisionmaker pursues but one standard of conduct. He knows that, by the law of averages, he will regain at some future time that which he may lose in occasional defeats. Self-confidence through decisive action becomes the propelling force. Action is the basis of success—inaction the basis of failure.

Making accurate decisions is not predicated on a foundation of luck and chance. They are a result of mental conditioning to think logically about the circumstances requiring a choice. When one's mind is attuned to think before acting then quick decisions or those requiring much study and research have a far better chance of producing good results. Following are a series of simple but important steps that can enhance your decision accuracy:

1. *Pursue high ideals*—there is no substitute for truth, fairness, justice, goodwill, quality. These represent standards, values. You may not always achieve your ideals, but like the stars above, they will serve as your guide. Do not forsake high ideals for mediocrity.

2. *Think, listen, read*—think objectively; thinking is your primary source of power; listening is your major source of OPE "Other people's experience"; reading is your foundation of wisdom. Each provides a fountain of ideas which, when thoughtfully considered, adds confidence and eliminates doubt. (Review how to "Analyze Your Problems" in Chapter 3.)

3. *Keep an open mind*—personal biases, hunches, pride of authorship, selfishness, are mental barriers to reality and the valued input of others. Flood your mind with facts, information, alternative possibilities and consequences—each source fortifies the best choice.

4. *Share your knowledge*—don't be afraid to talk freely about your ideas. Sharing opens the channel of ideas from others and the marriage of thoughts from two or more minds magnifies the potential manyfold. Remember—always give credit to others for their input.

5. *Make defeats a lesson*—consider temporary defeats a stumbling block in the pathway to success. A setback

or failure should not be viewed as the end—see it as a lesson, perhaps a blessing in disguise. Simply build a bridge over or around the obstacle and move forward.

6. *Walk with active faith*—decisions are the starting point toward unknown results and will be influenced by your degree of confidence. Thoughts of failure beget failure. Courage and the endurance of an active faith will overcome endless obstacles that try your patience and skill.

7. *Be loyal, true, frank*—these factors reveal dedication to the purpose for which your decision was made. Flippant, irresponsible decisions are usually without purpose, hence get little support.

8. *Take decisive, responsible action*—a well thought-out plan supported by a worthy purpose and ideal in responsible hands has the greatest chance of succeeding.

Each time you make a decision imagine that you are taking aim with a bow and releasing an arrow toward a target. Ask yourself: "Will it hit the bull's-eye, the outer circle of the target, or miss completely?" The chances of scoring a bull's-eye or landing in the target field will depend on several key factors: proper preparation, a decisive aim, adequate propelling power, responsible action, and active faith in end results. And so it is with making accurate decisions.

Delivery decisions identify the major and minor performers.

Build Confidence in Others

Do you reflect confidence in others?
People will join and follow you when they sense a degree of confidence in your ability and intentions. Or they will want you to join them because they feel your contributions will be mutually beneficial as in an employee–employer relationship. Ability alone will not generate success. It takes the support of people.

Confidence begets confidence—we seek those associations in which there is mutual trust. Unfortunately many associations do not always provide the ideal relationships for building such trust. For example the history of management–union relationships throughout the world is filled with accounts of mistrust, strikes, disagreement, grievances. The resultant disharmony has led to lower productivity. Automation and robots continue to supplant toiling hands to avoid the problems of dissenting people. Too, the history of many nations of the world reflect distrust, disputes, and seemingly endless wars, terrorism, and strife over economic, social, religious and related problems. Each incident presents a picture of hate, greed, indifference to the needs of people.

The English historian, Arnold J. Toynbee, said "The world's greatest need is mutual confidence. No human being ever knows all the secrets of another's heart. Yet there is enough confidence between mother and child, husband and wife, buyer and seller, to make social life a practical possibility. Confidence may be risky, but it is nothing like so risky as mistrust."

History's picture of the results of distrust and lack of confidence in others offers a vivid reflection of the mass of human suffering caused by poor relationships. Whether the picture you see is viewed as a mass of people or the few people that make up your day-to-day associations the image is the same. There can be no growth or progress in poor relationships with people.

"Everybody is somebody" was the title of a speech I listened to recently. The speaker, Dr. Dorothy Finkelhor, once a high school dropout, described what happened when told by a teacher that she did not have the ability to complete school. She believed the teacher and quit school. Later when told by her mother that she really had great potential she reentered school and in due time received a Ph.D.—and ultimately became president of a university. It is the somebodies in your circle of relationships at work, socially, and in all other activities that help you become a somebody or a nobody. The difference will be in the level of confidence that you create in others. Building confidence in others need not be a complex or difficult task. In the final analysis people will see you for "what you are" and therein lies the secret. These three words reflect your thoughts, actions, concerns, feelings, values, and everything you believe in or stand for. Since mutual confidence is without question paramount to achievement, consider then the key factors of influence:

1. *Things you think*—actions portray thoughts, so think well of others; they are a somebody worthy of respect.
2. *Things you say*—words reflect your attitude toward life and people; kindliness, encouragement, and reinforcement given to others makes them feel and act like a somebody worthy of your acquaintance.
3. *Things you do*—approach to all activities, the way you pursue work, overall competence, enthusiasm, goal orientation, values, sense of fairness, present a model of a somebody worthy of following.
4. *Things you share*—credit given, rather than credit taken is an unselfish trait of a somebody worthy of trust.
5. *Things you believe*—consideration of human dignity above pay, promotion, represent a model of a somebody that is fair and just.

Paul Tournier, Swiss psychiatrist declared "A lot of our behavior is determined by imputation—we tend to conform to what is expected of us." To have people in your midst that believe and trust you is an asset of great value. Their good thoughts reinforce your confidence. Too, they help keep your ideals alive. As with the stage performer, it is the approval of an audience, the applause, that ignites the fuel of stardom. Therefore, to assure your self-confidence, build the confidence of others through "what you are"—in everything you think, say, do, share, and believe—and help them become a somebody too.

Delivery confidence builds on confidence built in others.

And now a recapitulation of the ideas discussed in this chapter.

1. Self-confidence comes from the habit of accomplishment; confident thinking is rooted in habits. Underconfidence prevents success; overconfidence stimulates arrogance and leads to defeat.
2. Belief is a powerful force. Out of beliefs goals are achieved. Unlock the door to your confidence potential.
3. Strength, energy, coordination, and balance are rooted in an erect stance. Walk tall and think tall as you cross the three bridges to success.
4. Self-confidence to achieve follows the level of one's personal standards and remains at that level until the standards are raised.
5. Accomplishment is a result of making accurate decisions, good choices.
6. Confidence begets confidence. Consider that everybody is somebody—mutual confidence is simply helping others become a somebody too.

APOTHEGMS

1. *Delivery belief in ability assures accomplishment.*
2. *Delivery courage signifies confidence in end results.*
3. *Delivery standards are a gauge of excellence.*
4. *Delivery decisions identify the major and minor performers.*
5. *Delivery confidence builds on confidence built in others.*

13
Persistence Power

Success is to be measured not so much by the position one has reached in life as by the obstacles which he has overcome while trying to succeed.
—Booker T. Washington

(DELIVERY)

Do you persist when the going gets tough?

"A winner never quits, a quitter never wins"; "when the going gets tough, the tough get going." These two aphorisms are often quoted, especially in the sports world. Both reveal the reality of determination to succeed. Winning, successfully reaching a goal, completing a project, doing the impossible, is a result of persistence, stick-to-itivness. In fact few tasks are ever completed without ample measures of grit, patience, and perseverance.

Nothing in the world can take the place of persistence, suggested Calvin Coolidge. "Talent will not: nothing is more common than unsuccessful men with talent. Genius will not: unrewarded genius is almost a proverb. Education will not: the world is full of educated derelicts. Persistence and determination alone are omnipotent. The slogan 'Press On' has solved and always will solve the problems of the human race."

The greatest enemies of achievement are procrastination, vacillation, impatience, hesitation, despair. The person who is prone to hesitate over which of two projects he will pursue first will do neither. His mind is always open to a flood of intentions jumping from pillar to post, plan to plan. As a result he will never accomplish anything worthwhile.

Thomas A. Edison was asked by a reporter "Are your discoveries often brilliant intuitions? Do they come to you while you are lying awake nights?" He replied "I never did anything worth doing by accident nor did any of my inventions come indirectly through accident, except the phonograph. When I have definitely decided that something is worthy I go ahead and make trial after trial until it comes. Anything I have begun is always on my mind, and I am not easy while away from it until it is finished." This vivid explanation of Edison's working habits identifies clearly a key trait of his greatness—that of persistence.

Persistence power is an incredible force when continuously applied, but when relinquished good intentions simply drift like a ship without a rudder. The momentum of persistence power is like a fast rotating flywheel. It takes six times as much power to start a flywheel from a dead stop as it does to keep it going once in motion. In other words, it takes only one-sixth as much effort to keep going once you are on the way as it does to stop, then start again. When you are tempted to procrastinate or put off a worthwhile task until another time, remember the flywheel.

It is important to note that persistence power when applied to wrong solutions or actions will cause a lot of needless wheel spinning, waste resources, and even lead to disaster. Objectivity, realism, common sense, and talent are essential in the pursuit of worthwhile results. Merely beating your head against a wall is more likely to produce a concussion than a hole in the wall.

Achievers produce winning scores, top results, reach lofty heights, not by accident but by carefully laid plans and a burning catalyst of persistence to reach preset goals. In the poetic words of Longfellow:

The heights of great men reached and kept
Were not attained by sudden flight
But they, while their companions slept,
Were toiling upward in the night.

We have not wings, we cannot soar;
But we have feet to scale and climb
By slow degrees, by more and more,
The cloudy summit of our time.

Keep Your Battery Charged

Do you gain momentum before reaching the finish line?

The personal energy to start and finish a job or race comes from a single source—within you. The difference in those who sustain or gain momentum in approaching the finish line versus those who slacken or drop out is the level of energy in their human battery. That energy comprises many known ingredients such as drive, enthusiasm, ambition, motivation. There are some unknown electrons, molecules, and chemical compounds at work that reflect courage and spirit. The right combination of known and unknown elements serves to keep the human body at a peak charge and give forth maximum power.

The reason so few people achieve real success is the absence of energy to strive for excellence, or cross the finish line. Why? Excellence requires effort, often extra effort. Rundown batteries or those with a low charge simply do not have the umph or power to keep up the momentum for winning. Those who, for some reason, are unable or do not choose to keep their internal batteries at peak charge must be content with mediocrity.

People often assume that the energetic were born with ambition—they say it's something you either have or you don't. However, extensive studies on personal success do not agree. Ambition is an attitude, a frame of mind, which can change, often dramatically. A massive research project carried out by Harvard psychologist David McClelland (*Psychology Today* magazine, January, 1971), involved scholars in several nations and the study of children's literature of forty contemporary nations as well as ancient Greece and India. His studies revealed that achievement is more the result of education and culture than genetic inheritance.

McClelland says "People who are highly motivated tend to make excellent leaders. It's an efficiency kind of thing, but it also includes taking personal responsibility to solve problems and achieve moderate goals at calculated risks. People with a high need for achievement are not gamblers; they are challenged to win by personal effort, not by luck."

Persistent effort appears to be one of the most important ingredients for personal success. In Napoleon Hill's study of 500 of the most successful men in America, he found that great success was only won by people who overcame incredible obstacles and great discouragement. The common thread in each success story he said was "persistence."

J. C. Penney, founder of the well known department store chain stated that the secret of achievement can be found in the plain old habit of industriousness. In responding to the question: What makes genius tick? he said, "According to some authorities, it is not necessarily because they were gifted with phenomenal intelligence or mental powers. In fact, Dr. George Stoddard of New York University, an expert in the field has asserted that many children with near genius I. Q. scores are actually of mediocre intelligence. And according to a Stanford University study, many famous geniuses have not had unusually high I. Q.s.

What is the secret of their accomplishment, then? No one really knows for sure, but you will notice that industriousness—the capacity for grueling work plus the ability to immerse himself in whatever he is doing—is a common thread that is woven into the fabric of each and every top producer."

Geniuses themselves don't talk about the gift of genius; they just talk about work and long hours. As Edison said "Genius is 1 percent inspiration and 99 percent perspiration."

Others have said similar things in different ways:

Mark Twain: "The miracle or the power that elevates the few is to be found in their industry, application, and perseverance, under the prompting of a brave determined spirit."

Michaelangelo: "If people knew how hard I worked to get my mastery, it wouldn't seem so wonderful after all."

Alexander Hamilton (considered a financial wizard): "All the genius I may have is merely the fruit of labor and thought."

While hard work alone does not make a genius or spell success, there will be little success without it. Hard work requires maximum effort which, in turn, requires a highly charged battery.

How do you keep the human battery at peak charge to sustain maximum effort? It's so simple. Just attach your battery to the generator of your power resources, thus:

1. Mental power: constantly add to or renew your knowledge and experience.
2. Physical power: a continuous fitness program determines your strength, stamina, agility, coordination, endurance.
3. Social power: a deliberate effort to expand your interests through people increases the incentive to excel.
4. Spiritual power: daily involvement in spiritual renewal offers a limitless supply of God's goodness.

You now have the awareness to charge your battery to the maximum—the only limitations are those you impose. Have a worthy purpose in life and, having it, throw all the resource strength into your work that God has given you.

Delivery resources require continuous renewal.

Respond to Weaknesses

Do you improve weaknesses to avoid failure?

"No one is so strong as he who conquered weakness" wrote Elsa Barker. But what do you do about your strengths?

There is an age-old question: "To which should you devote the most development time, strengths or weaknesses?" Usually varied opinions are offered—some say strengths, others weaknesses. You could probably make a case for either depending on the stage of personal development and the goals you want to fulfill. But assuming your goals are based on the things you are reasonably qualified to do, then building on strengths and gradually developing weaknesses is the proper course.

For example, consider the golfer who has strengths in driving and chipping, but a weakness in putting. The professionals say "keep building on your strengths so they will increase, but devote more time to improving the weakness. Don't forsake strengths just to overcome a single weakness." The latter approach might only produce a strong weakling, that is, nothing would be done well.

Strengths and weaknesses are what you have and don't have, what you can do and can't do. Strengths are assets, weaknesses are liabilities. Strengths are like cash in the bank, weaknesses a debt—something you are obligated to overcome to be a great achiever. Drawing on the golfer's analogy, it is logical to build on what you have—the assets—and strive to overcome the liabilities or weaknesses. By reducing or paying off the debts of weakness, the major obstacle to your persistence power is eliminated.

Persistence can overcome virtually any kind of barrier, but weaklings give up easily in the face of obstacles. Nothing is more essential to success than the ability to stick to the project at hand. "People of mediocre ability," said Bernard Baruch "sometimes achieve outstanding success because they don't know enough to quit."

History reveals many names of great achievers that stand as a testimony of what can be accomplished when responding to weaknesses. Norman Vincent Peale said "When I started out from college I had the biggest inferiority complex that existed." As a young man he was so self-conscious and tongue-tied he was afraid to recite in class. He persisted and responded to his weaknesses and became one of America's most prominent preachers and authors.

The life story of Helen Keller reflects incredible accomplishments even though she was handicapped. She was blind and deaf from the age of two. "I thank God for my handicaps," said Helen. She gained worldwide fame for her aid to the handicapped, as an author and lecturer.

Ludwig Von Beethoven, beset with deafness in 1814 wrote some of his greatest music after becoming totally deaf in 1817. George Frederic Handel wrote *The Messiah* when he was in dire financial trouble and in poor health.

Winston Churchill had a serious speech impediment and was not considered a good writer. He responded to these weaknesses and became one of the most famous and oft-quoted speakers of the era. Author of histories, biographies, and memoirs, he was awarded the 1953 Nobel Prize in Literature.

Franklin Roosevelt, stricken with polio in 1921 served as President of the United States for the longest period in history, 1933 to 1945, from a wheel chair.

What are your weaknesses—those that influence your persistence power? When you have identified these limitations, then you must decide what you can and want to do about them.

There is great strength in weaknesses as can be seen from the aforementioned examples. It does take determination and belief in yourself to respond to them. Bob Richards, former Olympic pole vaulter, studied the success of hundreds of athletes. He found that 90 percent of the finest athletes were under 5'10" tall and weighed less than 185 pounds. He says the secret of their success was not great size or strength, rather their determination and absolute belief in themselves.

Delivery weaknesses, when conquered, are a source of great strength.

Concentrate on Best Results

Do you visualize the consequences of achievement?

The height of your persistence power is gauged by the depth of concentrated effort on achieving results. The greater your desire to succeed, the greater the degree of concentrated effort you will put forth. In other words, if your interest in being an effective employee, manager, sports competitor, artist, lawyer, or other position is high, then your willingness to concentrate on achieving excellence will be high. Low achievers have low ability to apply concentrated effort and are often pursuing many interests with limited results.

Concentration is the act of directing one's thoughts, efforts, strength, and intensity toward one idea, subject, or goal to achieve satisfactory benefits. It is the ability to control thoughts and actions, to finish things started. "Concentration is the secret of strength in politics, in war, in trade, in short in all management of human affairs" said Emerson. The philosophy of Elbert Hubbard portrays that "The difference in men does not lie in the size of their heads, nor in the perfection of their bodies, but in this one sublime ability of concentration—to throw the weight with the blow, live an eternity in an hour."

Consequences of concentrated effort are the benefits received. These may be great or small as challenges are overcome, races are won, or defeat occurs. There are lessons in both that contribute to experience and progress.

Three considerations can improve your power of concentration. First, realize that great achievement requires great effort. The higher a pinnacle or goal the more effort required. Worthwhile accomplishments are seldom easy. For instance, sport figures undergo long periods of development, continuous training, and endure many levels of competition to become champions. A classic case is that of Wilma Rudolph who started her life as a cripple. She was unable to walk before age six and then only with sheer determination to overcome. After struggling to walk she ultimately managed to run a little, but was slow and awkward at first. Finally she was able to run with other children and began to compete. Determined to succeed she persisted with practice and continued to enter competitive races. With concentrated effort and training, the help of a devoted coach, and a vision of being a champion she competed in the 1960 Olympics and won three gold medals.

A second consideration for improving your concentration and, in turn, your persistence power, is devotion to one idea or goal. A Spanish proverb says "If you would be Pope, you must think of nothing else." Drawing again on athletic feats, swimmer Mark Spitz was a favorite to win gold medals in the 1968 Mexico City Olympics, but the timely power to excel and fulfill predictions did not materialize. Determined to be a champion he set his sights on the 1972 Olympics scheduled to be held in Munich, W. Germany. With concentrated effort, and a determined spirit, he trained extensively, went prepared, and expected to win. He brought home not one, but seven gold medals.

During the February 1980 Winter Olympics in Lake Placid, New York, the U.S. Hockey Team gave an incredible demonstration of concentrated effort and devotion to one goal. The team, comprised of amateur minor league players and college players, stunned the world when they beat the reigning Olympic and world champion Soviet team in the semifinal round. Then went on to beat Finland in the finals for the gold medal.

The Nobel and Pulitzer prizes, Spingarn Medal, and other annual awards recognize people who have made major achievements for the good of humanity in journalism, literature, music, sports, education, and other fields. The recipients are invariably those who have concentrated on one primary endeavor. Field Marshall Erwin Rommel of WWII repute said: "One of the most important factors, not only in military matters, but in life as a whole, is the ability to direct one's whole energies toward the fulfillment of a particular task."

The third consideration is to concentrate on those parts of any task that will produce the greatest return. It is often frustrating and sometimes fruitless to focus on all aspects of a task. The theory of concentrating on major issues is commonly used in the business world and known as the Pareto Theory or 20–80 Principle. Wilfredo Pareto, an Italian economist applied mathematics to economic theory to differentiate rational and nonrational factors. The theory states that 20 percent of the factors will account for 80 percent of the results and 80 percent will contribute to only 20 percent of the results. This theory has been widely accepted and applied in such areas as sales, inventories, and production with uncanny accuracy. By using the 20–80 Principle you can be selective of those areas where concentrated effort offers the greatest return.

Keep the picture of the consequences of achievement in your mind, visualize end results. You will be continually inspired to concentrate on fulfilling that vision. It will take effort, devotion to one idea, and a selective approach to the areas that offer the greatest return.

Delivery concentration on best results produces highest benefits.

Be Patient

Are you a patient person?

The greatest servant of persistence power is patience; the greatest barrier is impatience. Emotional feelings arising from impatience can easily destroy the best laid plans as well as relations with all people involved. "All power is a component of time and patience" says an old proverb.

Patience is a human quality of inestimable value. The reward of patience always ranks at the top because of its significant effect on achieving results. The Apostle Paul, in his numerous writings to churches advised the Galatians "let us not become impatient in doing good, for at the proper time we will reap a harvest if we do not give up."

The value of patience in any venture has been proven time and time again, yet few people consciously apply these lessons of the past. Orison S. Marden wrote "patience is the guardian of faith, the preserver of peace, the cherisher of love, the teacher of humility. Patience governs the flesh, strengthens the spirit, sweetens the temper, stifles anger, extinguishes envy, subdues pride; she bridles the tongue, restrains the hand, tramples upon temptations, endures persecutions. Patience is the courage of virtue, enabling us to lessen pain of mind or body; it does not so much add to the number of our joys as it tends to diminish the number of our sufferings."

Patience allows you to increase your knowledge because it takes time to "be patient" and time provides the opportunity to think. There's a story about a wise old college president who, delivering a graduation address, said "Gentlemen, most of you will marry. Be kind to your wives. Be patient with them. When you are going out together, do not fret if she is not ready on time. Keep a good book handy. Read it while you wait. And, gentlemen, I assure you that you will be astonished at the amount of information you will acquire."

Significant achievements invariably unfold evidence of great perseverance and patience. Consider the pyramids in Egypt built nearly 4000 years before the time of Christ; Webster took thirty-six years to develop his dictionary; Bancroft spent twenty-six years on his "History of the United States"; Stephenson worked fifteen years on his locomotive; Watt spent twenty years on his condensing engine. Many of today's marvels in engineering, science, medicine, literature, art, music, and other fields are replete with examples. Advanced technology has shortened the time span for completing the most complex developments. Computer technology and space travel are but two examples. However, each great accomplishment will contain a fair measure of patience regardless of its complexity. It is said that only those who have the patience to do simple things perfectly will acquire the skill to do difficult things easily.

Patience is the ability to endure with calmness and self-control; impatience is an attitude that can be changed. Once a Quaker, calm and poised after a volley of bitter abuse, was asked how he conquered his impatience. He replied "Friend, I will tell thee. I was naturally as hot and violent as thou art. Yet, when I observed that men in passion always speak loud, I thought if I could control my voice, I should repress my passion. I have therefore made it a rule never to let my voice rise above a certain key. By careful observance of this rule I have, by the blessing of God, mastered my tongue."

Patience and tolerance are companions. One of the major problems for most people is intolerance of others' faults and weaknesses. We are often influenced by the thoughts that our ways, methods, choices, and suggestions are best. Yet, when we find it is impossible to accomplish much on our own and realize that the help of other people is essential, tolerance of their differences will be accepted.

To achieve a high level of patience I recommend adopting the four "T" approach. Think—Tongue—Tolerance—Temperament. Thinking stimulates new thoughts and solutions to difficult or frustrating experiences. The tongue can be as sharp as a two-edged sword; it merits careful use. Tolerance of others' faults and weaknesses makes us aware that we too are imperfect. Controlled temperament can move mountains, even if inspired by anger.

To develop an attitude of patience it is essential to adopt the right frame of mind. I suggest printing the word **PATIENCE** in large bold letters on several slips of paper. Then place them in strategic places such as on the bathroom mirror, or on the telephone where you will see them often. Each time you see the word, consciously consider the T—T—T—T approach, Think—Tongue—Tolerance—Temperament.

Learn patience from the lesson,—
Tho' the night be drear and long,
To the darkest sorrow there comes a morrow,
A right to every wrong.
            —John Townsend Trowbridge

Delivery patience is an attitude for greatness.

Never Despair

Do setbacks challenge you to take action?

Everyone has probably experienced spells of despondency as a result of setbacks, failures, disappointments, tough obstacles. Many have doubtless felt like throwing in the towel saying "It isn't worth it," "What's the use?" or "It's impossible." Some have literally thrown in the towel. These are not abnormal circumstances. Anyone may occasionally stumble, fall, or fail. The real challenge is to overcome, rebuild, keep trying, and move forward.

Baseball great Babe Ruth struck out 1330 times, but his 714 home runs completely obliterated the strikeouts. Cy Young, perhaps the greatest pitcher of all times actually lost almost as many games as he won. His record of 511 wins still stands today. The challenge to hit home runs, pitch winning games was the real motivation to move forward. Certainly the strikeouts and losses offered opportunities for despondency.

Despair is the arch enemy of progress, the thief of hope, melter of courage, scourge of belief, product of self-pity, the door to failure. It reduces persistence power to nil.

"No clear-thinking or clear-seeing man or woman can be an apostle of despair" declared Ralph Waldo Trine. "He alone fails who gives up and lies down. To get up each morning with the resolve to be happy; to take anew this attitude of mind whenever the dark or doleful thought presents itself, or whenever the bogeyman stalks into our room or crosses our path, is to set our own conditions to the events each day. To do this is to condition circumstances instead of being conditioned by them."

Action is the magic word—the key to overcoming any inclination to give up or to eliminate feelings of despondency. Two major steps are essential to conquer such feelings. First, determine the source. Second, take action. The culprit of influence is usually self-instigated; circumstances are self-generated. There may be pessimistic influence from prophets of doom, but whatever the source you will hold the power to change those thoughts that created the circumstances.

A group of sales personnel met to discuss declining sales volume and determine steps to improve the situation. Conversation filled the air with gloom about their plight and curiosity about the success of competitors. Finally one salesman said, "About all we seem to be doing is complaining and hanging crepe paper. Let's do something rather than talk in circles about our misery."

Action is the destroyer of despair, idleness its source. Thomas Carlyle offers a vivid picture: "There is perennial nobleness, and even sacredness in work. There is always hope in a man that actually and earnestly works; in idleness alone there is perpetual despair." One of the best tonics to stimulate action as well as health is work. It offers an opportunity for expression, growth, and to make a useful contribution. Any change in the environment will influence attitudinal change, if you let it. Take a walk in the woods and enjoy nature's landscape. Attend a good movie. Take a trip to your favorite camp site or lodge. Join others in light conversation, but do not talk about your troubles. Change the scenery and cleanse the negative thoughts from your mind. Find things to do that provoke happy thoughts. Happiness is the sunshine of the heart, the freshener of the mind.

Accept the challenge to take action when overcome by occasional setbacks and renewed persistence power will propel you forward again.

Delivery action is the tonic that conquers despair.

A reminder of some key points in each chapter section and listing of the apothegms will serve as a stimulus to use Persistence Power in your delivery system.

1. Nothing will take the place of persistence power, neither talent, genius, education. Persistence and determination alone are omnipotent.
2. Excellence requires effort, often extra effort. The reason so few people achieve real success is the absence of energy to strive for excellence.
3. Strengths and weaknesses are likened to your assets and liabilities—strengths are like cash in the bank, weaknesses a debt to overcome. There is great strength in weaknesses.
4. Concentration of effort is the secret of strength in all endeavors. The consequences are the benefits received.
5. Patience is a human quality of inestimable value. All power is a component of time and patience. It is an emotion that can be controlled; impatience is an attitude that can be changed.
6. Despair can reduce persistence power to nil, if you let it. Action is the magic word for overcoming despondency and despair. Condition the circumstances rather than be conditioned by them.

APOTHEGMS

1. *Delivery resources require continuous renewal.*
2. *Delivery weaknesses, when conquered, are a source of great strength.*
3. *Delivery concentration on best results produces highest benefits.*
4. *Delivery patience is an attitude for greatness.*
5. *Delivery action is the tonic that conquers despair.*

14

Success Power

> Our belief at the beginning of a doubt-
> ful undertaking is the one thing that
> insures the successful outcome of our
> venture.
>
> —William James

(ACHIEVEMENT QUOTIENT)

Do you believe you can raise your achievement level?

I anticipate that you really want to take steps to increase your AQ level as high as your talents and ability will allow. Otherwise you probably would not have read to this point. The above quotation about belief, by William James, is included here as a reminder that the strength of belief in yourself and your abilities to be successful is a key factor in any venture you may choose.

The course of travel outlined in previous chapters has covered all components of the achievement formula. These were: Compassion for people—Preparation for life's activities—Quality of effort—Delivery system for the end product, "you." The primary focus has been on ingredients for developing vital power resources and applying them in daily roles.

Upon completion of any journey such as a vacation, academic program, or simply reading a book, it is appropriate to sit back and reflect on how this new learning experience can be usefully applied in daily life. The chapter sections that follow represent a series of steps designed to guide and help you in systematically applying all components of the formula, that is, C (P + Q + D) = AQ. When the formula is applied, the results can lead you to a higher achievement quotient.

The words "when applied" perhaps need emphasis. An achievement formula will not produce results except with human effort. It is not a matter of reading, then expecting things to happen. You alone are the initiator, the instigator, the energy source necessary for forward motion. It is you that will make things happen in your life.

A retired business executive was once asked the secret of his success. He said it could be summed up in three words—"and then some." "I discovered at an early age," he declared, "that most of the difference between average and top people could be explained in three words. The top people did what was expected of them—and then some."

In addition he said "They were thoughtful of others, considerate and kind—and then some. They met their obligations and responsibilities fairly and squarely—and then some. They were good friends and helped neighbors—and then some."

Charles M. Schwab left a record of progressive achievement levels in his successful career with Bethlehem Steel Company. Like many success-oriented people he followed formulas or well defined guidelines for achievement. Here, for example, are his ten commandments for success—note each point starts with action words of what one should do:

1. Work hard. Hard work is the best investment a man can make.
2. Study hard. Knowledge enables a man to work more intelligently and effectively.
3. Love your work. Then you will find pleasure in mastering it.

4. Be exact. Slipshod methods bring slipshod results.
5. Do your best in all things. The man who has done his best has done everything. The man who has done less than his best has done nothing.
6. Have a spirit of conquest. Thus you can successfully battle and overcome difficulties.
7. Cultivate personality. Personality is to a man what perfume is to a flower.
8. Have initiative. Ruts often deepen into graves.
9. Help and share with others. The real test of business greatness lies in giving opportunity to others.
10. Be democratic. Unless you feel right toward your fellowmen you can never be a successful leader of men.

Virtually every successful person that I know or have read about throughout history has revealed a formula, set of commandments, or list of steps that he followed for progress and personal growth. It paved the way for many and it can do so for you. To help you achieve your desired level of progress and growth let us pursue Success Power in the manner which has served others so effectively.

Adopt Reasons for Achievement

Do you support your activities with sound reasons?

An old legend tells of a king and queen who were blessed with the birth of a son. Twelve fairies came and each gave the son a gift such as wisdom, beauty, strength. The twelfth gave the gift of discontent. The king was angry and drove her away. The prince grew with great promise, but manifested no disposition to develop his talents. There was no energy, no enthusiasm, no ambition in any of his endeavors. The discontented prince saw no reason to achieve, thus found himself without resource power for a worthwhile life. He merely chose to exist.

Reason is the cause, prime mover, incentive, motive, the mainspring for action. Without reasons to support our activities, we, like the prince, will merely exist. Energy, enthusiasm, ambition, turns to listlessness and indifference toward accomplishing anything worthwhile.

Success power stems from the thought process of worthy reasons and a devoted spirit to pursue any task with all your resources. Out of worthy reasons for achievement goals can be set. Out of goals action plans can be laid. Out of action plans tasks can be pursued, and obstacles can be surmounted, large or small, that lead to major accomplishments.

Don't underestimate the power of your personal input; after all it is your effort that is required to guide your growth.

A young artist, studying under a great master, came to the studio one day and asked permission to use his master's brush. The request was granted, and the man went happily on with his own painting, thinking that now his work would be much better. A short while later he returned with the brush, complaining that he could do no better with it than he could with his own brush. An assistant in the studio, hearing his complaint said, "Friend, it is not the master's brush you need, but the master's devotion, the master's spirit." And so it is with your achievements, it requires your devotion and spirit.

It is said that people with reasons for their actions seldom need excuses. Or, as Oliver Wendell Holmes aptly states: "Reason means truth and those who are not governed by it take the chance that some day the sunken fact will rip the bottom out of their boat." John Henry Cardinal Newman, in his Oxford University Sermons described reason or the excuse of reason, as "a living spontaneous energy within, not an art. All men have a reason," he said, "but not all men can give a reason."

If you were asked to make a list of all the reasons for doing the things that occupy your time, could you do it? Try; it may seem a difficult task at first, but in time a representative list will evolve. To make this an easy and logical task, consider classifying your reasons according to resource power. That is, separate them by mental, physical, social, and spiritual resources. For example under Mental: list reasons for knowledge and experience; Physical: recreation, sports, and similar activities; Social: include finance, job interests, home and family needs, community involvement and related items; Spiritual: Church, bible study activities, and other religious programs for self and family. The listing will no doubt be a revelation of your involvement, or lack of it, in worthwhile causes. In reviewing your list some functions may be difficult to really justify. The listing will serve to identify tasks where you might better spend more of your time.

It will pay dividends to apply the 20–80 Principle, described in Chapter 13, "Concentrate On Best Results," to your list. As in any activity you will discover approximately 20 percent of your effort is contributing 80 percent of the results. Since the remaining 80 percent will only be contributing about 20 percent to the total picture these items may offer a fertile area for reconsideration.

When the weeding out of superfluous activities is accomplished, study the remaining items and determine whether the present effort will get you where you want to go. If not, then consider pursuing new programs to fill in the voids and bring the development of your resources in balance with goals.

Back up your activities with sound, logical reasons and unleash the mainspring of action in everything you do. Young Emmet J. McCormack applied sound reasoning to his search for worthwhile employment and it lead to a great achievement. His father had died and it was necessary for him to earn a living for himself and his family. He tried to get a job as an office boy, but four successive firms had told him they didn't have enough work to keep a boy busy. After considerable thought, young McCormack went back to the firms, offering each of them one-fourth of an office boy. They hired him. McCormack later became co-founder of Moore-McCormack Lines, the second largest American flag-shipping company. He often told of how proud he was to have been the world's first "syndicated office boy."

Achievement Quotient rises when actions are supported with worthwhile reasons.

Commit Yourself to Do Great Things

Do you make your own opportunities?

Opportunities may come your way and they may not. The wise make their own and take advantage of every one that does come along which will serve to fulfill goals. It is fruitless to wait for a helping hand or some recruiter to pick you out of the masses and steer you to the ladder of success. The opportunities that you make, prepare for, and take advantage of are the ones that lead to achievement, not necessarily those that others may choose for you. A simple statement by Alexander Smith has great wisdom: "The greatness of an artist or a writer does not depend on what he has in common with other artists, but on what he has peculiar to himself."

Terry McCann, Executive Director of Toastmasters International, an Olympic gold medal winner and superachiever revealed his five-step plan for success (The Toastmaster, July 1981). "I had big dreams as a young boy growing up in Chicago," says Terry. "I was raised in a lower middle-class Polish neighborhood, and my family, like others on our block, lived with the hope of someday finding a better life in the suburbs. Our people were tough. They worked hard, sometimes holding down as many as three jobs. They never took vacations—there were too many mouths to feed. During the summer, the boys in my neighborhood only had time for sports. We loved competition and winning was everything in our little society."

"I was determined to be a winner and get ahead, and I knew my ticket to the suburbs was a college education. But I wanted more than that. In high school, I discovered wrestling. When I learned it was part of the Olympic curriculum, I wanted to compete with the best wrestlers in the world—and win. I didn't take my eyes off that goal until I stood on the winner's platform in Rome in 1960 and accepted my Gold Medal."

Terry says that in the years leading up to that great moment he learned a lot about what it takes to be an achiever—it meant:

- Making the most of your talent and ability.
- Pouring every ounce of your power into every effort.
- Doing something better than it's ever been done before.
- Knowing where you should end up in life.
- Setting challenging but attainable goals.
- Leaving the world better than you found it.
- Having a keen sense of competition.

McCann's five-step plan for success is: (1) Think and act like a pro. (2) Reach beyond your grasp. (3) Make a mission—goals—action plan. (4) Concentrate on major efforts. (5) Catch the third wave. The latter step stems from Terry's experience as an avid surfer. He discovered that waves generally come in sets of three. He says "The third wave is usually the biggest and the best. It's the one with the most energy and power. To catch it, you have to be in the right place at the right time. As you see it on the horizon, you paddle to the point of pickup. Then, as it surges toward the beach, you use all the arm and shoulder power you can muster to thrust yourself forward. You can't hold back. You have to go for it with all your skill and strength. Your reward is the thrill of coasting up and down the swell and feeling the tranquillity of a smooth ride. There's nothing like it. But you get the chance to ride that wave the same way you reach many achievements in life—by being in the right place at the right time and taking advantage of every opportunity. You can also make opportunities by following this five-step formula for achieving."

Man's achievements are an unending story of determination to improve his position in life. Evidence the growth from caves to skyscrapers—wooden-wheeled carts to space travel—slavery and serfdom to freedom—smoke signals to communication satellites—yes, even dreams to gold medals.

Each day unfolds new and greater innovations to replace the old or obsolete, the result of man's effort to make and take advantage of opportunities. Great achievers seldom accomplish anything by accident, rather as a result of commitment to a purpose, to do great things, to reach perfection, to serve others.

Michelangelo was working on a statue one afternoon when some friends visited him. A month later they returned and found him still working on the same statue. "What have you done since our last visit?" one asked. "Oh, I've smoothed a line here, and polished an arm, taken a few flakes of marble from the forehead, and so on," replied the great artist. "But those are only trifles! Is that all you've done?" "True, but trifles make perfection, and perfection is no trifle."

Opportunities are available for the maker; greatness is but a seed planted in the mind of one who is committed to do great things.

Achievement Quotient rises with a commitment to greatness.

Fulfill Your Aspirations

Is desire to excel a habit with you?

Within the depths of your mind lie the cravings of your fondest desires, the spiritual elevators of mind and body that can fulfill worthy dreams and ambitions. Man achieves that to which he aspires. His longing is the barometer of what he can be.

Peter Cooper was denied ordinary school privileges. He tried to find night school programs that would allow him to continue learning his trade by day and study at night. There were few night schools in that era. With deep disappointment in his heart, he said, "If ever I prosper in business so as to acquire more than I need, I will try to found an institution in the city of New York, where apprentice boys and young mechanics shall have a chance to get knowledge in the evening."

Peter learned to make hats, as a young boy, following his father's trade. Then he got a job as an apprentice carriage-maker and worked four years learning the trade. He had an innovative mind and made a machine for mortising hubs which proved very profitable for his employer.

About the time he finished his apprenticeship the carriage business faded. But there was a demand for cloth and for machinery for its manufacture. Peter invented a machine for cutting the nap on cloth and could not make enough to satisfy the demand. In time the demand for his machines ceased. He turned to cabinet-making, but was not successful. He then bought a grocery store and was doing well when he was offered an opportunity to buy a glue factory for two thousand dollars. The business became a success. Peter invested surplus cash in land. Still using his innovative mind he found time to build a locomotive that became a success.

At age sixty Peter Cooper had accumulated seven hundred thousand dollars above the capital in his various enterprises. By this time evening schools were established in many locations. He heard of the Polytechnic School of Paris. This seemed to trigger that long sought-after aspiration that he held in his mind. As a result Cooper Union was built as a free gift to the city of New York, on the site of his old grocery store at a cost of seven hundred thousand dollars. He continued to serve as a prime benefactor and contributed a total of two million dollars.

When Cooper Union opened its doors, two thousand young people applied for admission. Thousands have since graduated from this fine institution—once only an aspiration in the mind of Peter Cooper. That was over 100 years ago. But Cooper Union exists today. Its students are among the most select in the country in such fields as Engineering, Science, Art, Architecture.

Man is known to give his greatest mental and physical

effort and devotion to fulfilling long sought-after ambitions. Successful businessmen, artists of renown, authors of fame, sports figures of acclaim, stars of stage and screen, reflect a common denominator—the habit of striving to fulfill their deepest aspiration. What is it that makes them different from the ordinary person? It's doing what those of lesser accomplishments do not want to do. That is, making a habit of striving to be the best in their field.

Great success is achieved by the minority who choose to be different. The successful minority are influenced by the desire to fulfill aspirations and produce results that please. The majority are influenced by the desire to accept what is—to be satisfied with whatever results they can obtain by doing the simple easy things laid out for them.

Your single most important qualification for success will be acquired through habit. When habits to achieve in any endeavor are formed, habits will form the future and the future holds the results of your aspiration. If you fail to form good habits that lead to excellence, then you will unconsciously be following habits that lead in other directions.

As you seek to fulfill your fondest dreams and aspirations consider deeply the potential end results. In the words of Ida Scott Taylor: "It is well to have longings and aspirations, to have ambitions and desires, but right should inspire them, truth govern them, and self-control keep them in check. Above all, let us hold fast to the hand of God, lest we go beyond His guidance, and forget that without Him no good is worth striving for. He will show us the right way, and help us to walk in it, if we only trust His guidance."

> Heaven is not reached at a single bound;
> But we build the ladder by which we rise
> From the lowly earth to the vaulted skies,
> And we mount to its summit round by round.
> —Josiah Gilbert Holland.

Achievement Quotient rises with the habit of striving for excellence.

232

Pursue Worthwhile Ventures

Are you making the most of your potential?

The most logical way to achieve success is to find and develop ventures that are worthwhile. What could be more simple? But life and success usually turn out to be more complex, often because of our own indecision. Or perhaps we await the offer of a magic potion or a genie to pop up and fulfill our fondest dreams.

Legend says that when Solomon received the gift of an emerald vase from the Queen of Sheba, he filled it with an elixir which only he knew how to prepare. One drop was supposed to prolong life indefinitely. A dying criminal begged for a drop of the precious liquid, but Solomon refused to prolong the life of a criminal. When good and honorable men asked for it, they were refused or put off. Solomon preferred not to open the vase for just one drop. When Solomon himself became very ill he asked his servants to bring him the vase. He opened it and found the contents had evaporated. And so it is for those who wait in hopes of having a surefire venture laid in their hands.

In any moment of introspection one might think of many suggestions for beneficial ventures. But who is to say what is best for you? Only you will make the choice, perhaps in concert with others, about what is considered worthwhile and what is not. There is no exact set of rules. However, it often helps to have guidance to stimulate thoughts for oneself. Here are five steps that can be helpful in any venture. They are not intended to be inclusive for anyone, but should be helpful to everyone.

1. CONSIDER OPE (OTHER PEOPLE'S EXPERI-
   ENCE): Before launching into a venture it is wise to consider OPE and avoid repeating mistakes of the past. Some two thousand years ago Marcus Cicero, Roman orator, politician, philosopher, listed his "Six Mistakes of Men." They are relevant today:

- The delusion that individual advancement is made by crushing others.
- The tendency to worry about things that cannot be changed or corrected.
- Insisting that the thing is impossible because we cannot accomplish it.
- Refusing to set aside trivial preferences.
- Neglecting development and refinement of the mind and not acquiring the habit of reading and study.
- Attempting to compel other persons to believe and live as we do.

Failures and mistakes serve as the best teachers. But success generally accrues to those who make the greatest profit from the fewest mistakes. Therefore do not approach your choice of venture with the fear of failure—that could be your greatest mistake. It is not a sin to fail or make mistakes. It is certainly the beginning of the end to repeat mistakes. What does matter is that you learn from them and do something to correct them. "Life is like an onion," suggested Carl Sandburg, "You peel off one layer at a time and sometimes you weep."

2. CONSIDER THINGS THAT INVOLVE OR BENEFIT OTHERS: Activities that utilize the efforts of people to produce a product or render a service offer great potential for many reasons. Worldwide unemployment alone signals a vital need for people to be usefully occupied. People are beneficiaries of the products that people produce or utilize. Small or large industry and business ventures are competitive and as a result, offer rewards for good products and services. This creates people satisfaction, both for the producer and user. It also punishes the noncompetitive, the producer of poor quality, and the inefficient.

Social services, recreation, and entertainment consume a great portion of leisure time of the vast majority.

Wherever people are involved or can benefit from a product or service you offer there is opportunity for success.

3. PURSUE HONEST MOTIVES: There is no substitute for personal integrity, honesty of purpose. Deliberate action to take advantage of people and satisfy selfish motives of greed, lust, or other reasons is the road to defeat. There are no rewards for dishonesty, fraud, falsehood. Only degradation and punishment.

4. BRING PEOPLE INTO YOUR CONFIDENCE: The fruits of your efforts can only be expanded through others. This is the first lesson that men and women learn as they enter the field of management. Their ultimate success depends on the ability to get work done through others. Too, a manager soon learns that confidence begets confidence. He must share with and generate faith and trust in people. In turn, followers respond to an atmosphere of confidence and work to achieve beneficial results for all. Therefore, follow the experience of successful managers. Work confidently with people to make your venture mutually beneficial.

5. TRUST IN GOD: The power of God is omnipresent, infinite. He has equipped you for life, but lets you decide what you want to be. It is said that, as the sun creates your shadow, God creates your soul, but in each case it is you who determines the shape. God is good, God is all, hence there can be no other results when you trust in His guidance. "If a sparrow cannot fall to the ground without His notice, is it probable that an empire can rise without His aid?" asked Benjamin Franklin.

Worthwhile ventures come in many types, sizes, and shapes. I believe that the simple, tried-true, ordinary, uncomplicated, pursuits offer the best potential especially for the beginner. Whatever your choice may be you will find, as many do, that the most successful ventures are those that give you the greatest enjoyment. After all, life is to be enjoyed.

Achievement Quotient rises when human potential produces greatest enjoyment.

Set Five-Year Growth Plans

Are your future plans in written form?

At this point you probably have a fairly clear idea of the things you would like to do to achieve desired growth for yourself and your dependents. From your reading and study to date it should be clear that goal setting, action planning, and implementing such plans are three essential steps for accomplishing your aims. I shall inject one additional thought: Personal growth and development of your resources does not happen overnight—it takes time, often a long time. But you already know that. I mention it here to help you appreciate the need for short- and long-range planning. I consider any task that cannot be completed in six months to be long range.

Today most successful businesses pursue five-year growth plans. Some plan twenty years ahead. It may sound presumptuous to think that any organization can predict where they will be in twenty years. The fact is, they can't with high accuracy. However, it offers the opportunity to do creative planning, to make things happen, to take advantage of or adjust to changes that will contribute to growth. Regardless of the length of growth plans, five or twenty years, adjustments are made annually or more often, if necessary, to factor in new events. Thus, the plans continually reflect an on-going picture of short-term and anticipated long-term results.

Picture yourself as a business entity. You possess relevant characteristics. For example, you are a body of knowledge, experience, skills—these represent a marketable product. Just as a product needs a consumer you need a user of your services or output and, in turn, require remuneration.

Thus, you—the product—generate income, incur operating expenses, pay taxes, make a profit or saving. When viewed in this manner the need for a growth plan is as vital to your success as it is to that of any company such as IBM, GE, or the local grocer. Picture yourself as president of one of those companies—would you expect to have your corporate growth plans in writing for all employees? Now picture yourself as president of your company—"you."

With you or the product in view what can you do to generate growth? Consider what the company or business might do. They will probably develop their organization, product lines, and marketing capabilities as they grow. You can do the same thing. Develop your organization resources, yourself "the product," and your marketing interests as the need for your services grow.

Consider now the areas of your development potential. I have indicated in earlier chapters that there are four areas that comprise your total resources and represent you "the product." These are mental—physical—social—spiritual resources. With these four factors again in view it will be relatively easy to develop a five-year growth plan.

The first step is to put pencil to paper, not just to think about it. Remember you are President of a company. Thomas Watson, father of IBM and long-time President and Chairman had a favorite aphorism: "If you want to be a big company tomorrow you have to start acting like one today." So let's start with paper and pencil and act like the successful ones do—write out your five-year growth plan. Start by asking yourself, "What are my five-year plans?" for:

Mental: Include knowledge, skill and experience necessary to meet your product and marketing requirements.

Physical: List steps required to get in shape and stay in shape.

Social: Identify requirements for a happy life; include education of family, relationships with

237

others, expansion of circle of friends, involvement in community affairs, etc.
Assess income needs, expenses, investments, savings.
Spiritual: List the activities you will pursue to fulfill
spiritual expression.

Now identify the things you will accomplish in each of
the five years. Don't try to force completion of everything
in one year—that seldom works. Pace yourself so as to enjoy
life as you grow. Savor your progress with the happy realization that you planned it. Many may think "how lucky you
are." But you can say "I planned to be lucky."

Writing out your five-year growth plan is a giant step. It
will all be for nought unless it is referred to daily and modi-
fied regularly to take advantage of unexpected changes as
they occur. In other words, promotion, new job opportunities, investment potential may occur faster than projected.
I suggest you adopt a specific time each day to look over
your plan. By so doing you are feeding your mind with a
definite plan. Regular reviews lead to habits; habits stimulate
desire and the determination to excel. Success power can
unfold for you just as it has for the many businesses that
use, constantly review, and update their long-term growth
plans.

*Achievement Quotient rises when growth plans are com-
mitted to writing.*

Launch Your Ship

Are you ready to reach out for higher pinnacles?
The preceding chapters set forth steps and methods for
applying your innate power to excel. Now it is time to apply
these procedures and re-decide, if necessary, in favor of your
real potential. It is one thing to read and think about your
future, to ponder what might have been or could be; it is
quite a different matter to take off into new horizons, blast

away from the launching pad and apply what you have learned.

Your experience to date may be likened to the "Parable of the Eagle." A farmer, while walking through the fields, found a young eagle. He took it home and put it with his chickens where it soon learned to behave like a chicken. One day a naturalist who was passing by, asked the farmer why an eagle should be confined to live in a barnyard with the chickens. The farmer replied, "Since I placed it with the chickens it has adopted their habits and never learned to fly. It simply behaves like a chicken." The naturalist said, "Since it has the heart of an eagle, it can surely be taught to fly." So the two men agreed to find out. The naturalist gently cradled the eagle in his hands and said, "You belong to the sky and not to the earth. Spread your wings and fly." But the eagle was confused. He did not know who he was or his potential. Seeing the chickens eating their food, he jumped down and joined the chickens.

The naturalist was determined. The next day he took the eagle up on the roof of the house and repeated the command, "You are an eagle, spread your wings and fly." But the eagle was afraid of the world around him and once again jumped down and joined the chickens. On the third day, the naturalist decided to take the eagle to a higher peak, this time a high mountain. He held the bird high and again encouraged him saying, "You are an eagle, spread your wings and fly; you belong to the sky and not to the earth." The eagle looked back at the barnyard, then up to the sky. Still he did not fly. Then the naturalist lifted him straight towards the sun; the eagle began to tremble, then slowly he stretched his wings. At last, with a triumphant cry, he soared away to higher and higher peaks.

The eagle, as far as anyone knows, never returned to the barnyard to lead the life of a chicken. He discovered his real potential and flew to greater heights. Just like the eagle, you can learn to think in terms of your real potential. You can, by applying the techniques learned in this book, ignite your energy-laden resources, release the stabilizing lines from your launching platform and soar like the eagle.

As you launch your ship toward new and wider horizons, be conscious of the myriad of controls at your fingertips. As in a space ship, you are in charge and have control of the directions and height you will soar. But you will not be without the influence of those at the space control center and observation stations around the world. A successful venture will depend very much on your relationship with all those who work closely with you and help you achieve. You will always be surrounded by interested observers who are constantly reporting on your position.

Most people seek guidance and assurance that their approach to new ventures will succeed, but in each instance they quickly discover that words of advice serve only as vital training. The actual pursuit is controlled by the individual. In 1692 a treatise titled *Desiderata* was found in Old Saint Paul's Church in Baltimore. Those who sought advice and comfort found it in the message. Oddly enough the same advice is as appropriate today as it was nearly 300 years ago. The message read: "Go placidly amid the noise and haste and remember what peace there may be in silence. As far as possible without surrender be on good terms with all persons. Speak your truth quietly and clearly; and listen to others, even the dull and ignorant; they too have their story. Avoid loud and aggressive persons, they are vexation to the spirit. If you compare yourself with others, you may become vain and bitter; for always there will be greater and lesser persons than yourself. Enjoy your achievements as well as your plans. Keep interested in your own career, however humble; it is a real possession in the changing fortunes of time.

Exercise caution in your business affairs; for the world is full of trickery. But let this not blind you to what virtue there is; many persons strive for high ideals; and everywhere life is full of heroism. Be yourself. Especially, do not feign affection. Neither be cynical about love; for in the face of all aridity and disenchantment it is as perennial as the grass.

Take kindly the counsel of the years, gracefully surrendering the things of youth. Nurture strength of spirit to shield you in sudden misfortune. But do not distress yourself with imaginings. Many fears are born of fatigue and loneliness. Beyond a wholesome discipline, be gentle with yourself.

You are a child of the universe, no less than the trees and the stars; you have the right to be here. And whether or not it is clear to you, no doubt the universe is unfolding as it should. Therefore be at peace with God, whatever you conceive Him to be, and whatever your labors and aspirations, in the noisy confusion of life keep peace with your soul. With all its sham, drudgery, and broken dreams, it is still a beautiful world. Be careful. Strive to be happy."

Achievement Quotient rises with preparation for new horizons.

Make Happiness Your Pilot

Are you truly happy in your vocation?

The people who achieve the highest level of satisfaction from their efforts will most likely be those who thoroughly enjoy the pursuit of their work or goal as though it were a hobby. Few hobbies are economic necessities; they are pursued for the enjoyment and satisfaction received. Would you be willing to pursue your job if it were not an economic necessity? Therein lies the secret of happiness in work—the happy worker is a productive worker. Since it may not always be practical to change jobs until finding the ideal happiness level, one must face the reality of creating his own contentment and joy. Start by making it your business to be happy—as with your hobbies—and you are bound to find happiness in business.

Many formulas for a happy life at work or play have been handed down over the years. Here are six rules that offer worthwhile directions. Let them serve as your pilot and enjoy their rewards:

1. Pursue a well-defined purpose. Happiness comes to those who have a purpose in life that they can pursue

each day with the intention of accomplishing something worthwhile. The greatest satisfaction comes from knowing that your efforts will be of value and appreciated by your family, employer, associates, and yourself— probably in that order. Work, even hard laborious work, need not be drudgery. Only our thoughts make it so.

2. Take responsibility for your own action. Being capable of standing on your own feet and feeling the responsibility to perform good work offers a sense of freedom— the liberty to judge your own efforts and strive to fulfill standards of excellence. It is action, responsible action, that creates happiness. Disraeli said, "Action may not always bring happiness, but there is no happiness without action."

3. Maintain respect for other people. Life is a system of relations with people, not an independent existence. Happiness comes from the realization that whatever one's job or hobby may be, the results of one's efforts are dependent in some way on others. The joy of this emotional feeling is a by-product of respect for others.

4. Be a self-starter. The person who waits for direction to work or requires very close supervision just to be kept busy is obviously not overly happy or productive. The discontented worker is the creator of his own unhappy circumstances. It is the self-created, happy environment, the love of duty that brings contentment.

5. Learn to live with ups and downs. It is not likely that every day of one's productive life will render bumper results. There will occasionally be stumbling blocks, declines in output, even failures. Happiness can be found in either ups or downs: one from the good fortune of producing satisfactory results, the other through faith and ability to recover. In either instance, you are the creator of happiness.

6. Stay close to God. Closeness to Him provides enduring happiness, the opportunity to share your thoughts, the

assurance of divine protection and guidance, a constant source of spiritual power in successes and failures.

By applying the above rules in your day-to-day activities you can become the creator of your own happiness—it will serve as your pilot. Do not fall victim to becoming a creature of circumstance.

Achievement Quotient rises with the creation of satisfying circumstances.

Keep Your Eyes on the Little Things

Do you consider all components of new projects?
Whether your venture be small or large there will invariably be several components that make up the end result. I have seen and been involved in several potential successes that turned to failure because the focus was totally fixed on the big things. Forgotten were the little pieces that, when joined together, made up the big ones. It is a fact of life that we often become more concerned with the taste of success than the slow process of planning, preparing, mixing, blending, and molding the ingredients into their intended form.

How many sour experiences can you recall that might have been avoided had you considered the little things? An empty gas tank, a dead car battery, bald tires gone flat, traveling the wrong road without a map, leaving home without money, lunch, umbrella, glasses, briefcase, or other necessity, omitting the baking powder from those homemade biscuits, the spices from the favorite sauces. Or consider some of the catastrophic construction incidents, building failures, auto accidents, plane crashes. Many, if not most, are attributable to human failings that, in many instances, could have been avoided by checking on the little things—taking precautionary measures.

"Count your pennies and the dollars will take care of themselves" is an old but realistic maxim. Or, to paraphrase Joel Weldon, popular speaker and seminar leader from

Phoenix, Arizona: "Elephants don't bite. What does bite us, or get to us, are the little things—those gnats and mosquitoes. The solution to improved performance is to do the 'little things' better, and then you will get the big ones right." The same philosophy is applicable to any business or personal venture. The successful pursuit of either is dependent upon the little parts that make up the whole venture.

Frustration abounds when a piece is missing from a jigsaw puzzle, a screw from an unassembled toy, the button from a new coat or dress. Why, then, are we not more conscious of similar failings in our big ventures? Perhaps, because of oversight, or thinking someone else will take care of the small ingredients, or because our primary concern is with the big pieces.

Let's face it! The successes of your projects are totally dependent upon you regardless of the number of pieces involved. Therefore, it behooves you to set up checklists, benchmarks, test procedures, trial runs, and other essential methods to insure that all components fit together and work before being assembled into the final product. This approach can be and is applied to something as small as a homemade cake, as significant as taking a vacation, or as large as the launching of a rocket. It was, you may recall, a small defective battery that delayed the initial launching of the space ship Columbia. It is, after all, the total ingredients that comprise an end result.

It is said that few business failures result from lack of capital. More often they are attributed to poor management savvy and the inability to control the key elements such as inventory, sales, operating expenses, customer relations— the many little pieces that comprise the whole.

"The creation of a thousand forests is in one acorn," said Emerson. A teakettle singing on the stove inspired the invention of the steam engine; a lantern swinging in a tower gave rise to the pendulum; an apple falling from a tree led to the discovery of the law of gravity. Little things lead to the creation of great things.

A stonemason building a wall was asked why he used

so many small stones along with the large ones. He replied, "These stones are like men. Many small men, like me, are needed to keep the big ones in place. If I leave the small ones out, the big ones will not stay in place, and the wall will fall. Many big men forget this and their walls will fall down."

Support your ventures, however large or small they may be, with appropriate checklists or other means so that you personally can insure the little pieces will not be left out. Failures may occur in the best laid walls—the reason will often prove to be the absence of those little stones. Success is most likely to occur when adequate checks are made to insure the little stones are in place.

Achievement Quotient rises when all the little details are accounted for.

Build a Success Consciousness

Do you have the will to succeed?

The seeds of success must be implanted deep in your mind and constantly nurtured to produce an unshakable willpower. Your will is the faculty of conscious and deliberate actions. It is the power source of determination; craving, longing, freedom to do what you most want to do. You may call it backbone, grit, guts, courage—the underlying influence to succeed is willpower.

Your goals represent the spirit of life. Willpower fuels that spirit and absorbs energies. The French language calls this spirit of life "élan vital," a harmonious phrase of two words, but it says so much. Goals, when influenced by a strong will, become fixed ideas, a mental plan. Here again the French language offers two more harmonious words, "idée fixe." The "élan vital" reflects the seriousness of your intent, the "idée fixe" your will or determination.

High achievers of yesterday and today have related many stories about how they built a consciousness in their minds before they built a fortune or pedestal of acclaim. Ford built a mental consciousness of success in motor cars then built a fortune; Edison built his inventions; Penney in merchandising; Kennedy in politics and government. "Élan vital" and "idée fixe" formed a pattern of harmony and success.

A young man in boot camp was receiving lengthy, passionate letters from his girlfriend. She loved him so much. Oh, if she could just see him, what she wouldn't do. With a strong "élan vital" and "idée fixe" he took off from the barracks, without a permit, running as fast as he could toward the camp exit. The gate guard saw him coming, knew he probably did not have a leave permit and cried out, "Halt! Halt!" Without missing a stride the young man shouted, "My mother is in heaven, my papa's in hell, and my girl is in Chicago—and I'm seeing one of them tonight!" He harbored a well-nurtured, unshakable willpower.

Several years ago, a bespectacled little girl, many pounds overweight, sat in a Sunday school class listening to a speech by an Olympic gold medalist. She kept jumping up and down saying, "I'm going to be a great tennis champion." No one in their wildest imagination could visualize that happening. But she could. And it did. Yes, that little girl carried a determined spirit and a fixed idea in her mind. Today she ranks among the greatest of all women tennis champions; her name—Billie Jean King.

An eight-year-old boy used to say, "I am going to be the greatest baseball catcher that ever lived." His mother told him, "That's impossible." When he graduated from high school, the Superintendent stopped him and said, "Tell the audience your future plans." "I am going to be the greatest baseball catcher that ever lived." The audience snickered. Today they applaud Johnny Bench who, in the minds of many, is probably the greatest baseball catcher who ever lived.

Many have built a success consciousness, then built riches. Why not follow the patterns of the achievers? You can if you have the spirit to do so and the will to fuel that spirit. Here are six things you can do to help build and fortify your success consciousness:

1. Make it a habit to think success. I believe that writing things down on paper or 3" x 5" cards and carrying them with you is an easy way to keep ideas in the forefront. They serve as frequent reference tools and help develop thinking habits. Use whatever convenient method suits your workaday style—the main thing is to develop the habit of thinking success about your goals and interests.
2. Read and study financial papers, stock markets, related books. Become familiar with the source and flow of riches; eliminate the fears of unfamiliarity. Money is, after all, the primary medium of exchange that leads to financial security. To get it you need to understand it, where it comes from and how to use it.
3. Study the methods great achievers have followed. There are no exact patterns that suit everyone, but you will discover the precise elements covered in this book are the key. Additionally, draw on the myriad of available educational sources and the practical experience of the successful, then adopt those ideas that best suit your goals. Virtually any information you want or need is available—try your library; make personal contacts with successful people, for example, bankers, brokers, business and industry leaders, city and government officials, lawyers, clergy, friends.
4. Dream a little. Let your imagination wander. Who has not built dream castles in his mind and filled them with aspirations? Have fun. Dream about the riches of money, security, health, happiness, that await you. It will serve to fuel the spirit of your will.
5. Discover your unique factor. Search your mind, talents, and abilities for the one unique factor that you possess and build on it.
6. Believe in your ability to succeed. If you think you can, you can. If you think you can't, you won't. Avoid negativism. There is no room in success consciousness for negative thoughts. They are like a dripping water

faucet—it will drive you crazy if you let it. Fix it. Think success, not failure.

You already possess the foundation for building a success consciousness. The world awaits. Apply yourself. Do it!

Achievement Quotient rises with the level of success consciousness.

Use Power Wisely

Do you share achievement rewards with others?
You have in your possession some of the greatest sources of power known to man. Fourteen have been presented; their application and use discussed. The sources are not new. They merely need reviving and activating to put you on the list of high achievers.

"Life is action, the use of one's powers," said Oliver Wendell Holmes. "As to use them to their height is our joy and duty, so it is the one end that justifies itself." Power is revealed in many ways. The artist reveals his through a brush; the musician blends sounds and harmonies; a mother shares love and affection for her family; a leader through guidance and development of people; an entertainer through the use of unique talents, skills, abilities; the scientist through new discoveries; the surgeon through life-saving measures. Of course, the awesome power of war and all its sophistication of guided missiles with the destructive warheads represent man's determination to defend or destroy himself. The power of storms, floods, earthquakes, and fire are among the several gigantic destructive forces—but these are, in most instances, beyond man's control. In this book we are dealing with power that is used for the growth, peace, and prosperity of mankind.

Personal power may be used constructively for the benefit of self and humanity in general. Or it may be used destructively to exploit or destroy humanity for selfish gains. There is but one intended use herein—for personal development, for sharing the many benefits with those who help you climb your achievement ladder and for sharing with humanity in general.

Let us re-examine the achievement formula, C (P + Q + D) = AQ, and then consider the fourteen sources of power that comprise it are the root structure of the "Tree Of Life" and its abundant potential:

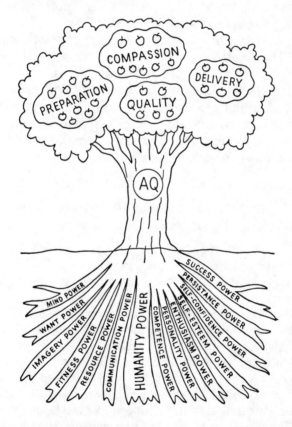

Humanity is represented as its primary and deepest root. It reaches down into the realms of compassion for people and receives nourishment and growth. Without this main root, the tree, like any tree in the forest, would be unstable, its growth stunted and subject to the perils of winds, storms, or just being crowded out by the faster growth of competitive trees that smother its lifelines.

The fibrous roots of the trees are represented by the thirteen subordinate power sources. They serve to fix the tree in place and feed it with riches of the surrounding environment. Each root requires ample quantities of food, water, and fertilizer for continuous growth and production. When feeding stops, the tree will wither and die.

Success is represented by the fruits of a well-nourished tree. The greater the compassion for its existence, its care and feeding, the greater will be the rewards.

Your use of power can be beneficial and rewarding. It can be harmful and degrading. A fine line separates these consequences. Use power wisely. Don't abuse it. The rewards for its thoughtful application are many as you strive to reach a higher level of achievement.

Achievement Quotient rises when life's rewards are shared.

The key points in Chapter 14 and the apothegms are listed below for your review.

1. The strength of belief in yourself and your abilities to be successful is a key factor in any venture.
2. There must be reason to achieve. Reason is a primary moving force.
3. Join the wise and make your own opportunities; take advantage of every opportunity that comes along which helps to fulfill your goals.
4. Uncover those worthy dreams and aspirations. Successful people make a habit of striving to fulfill their deepest aspirations.
5. Find and develop ventures that are worthwhile. Do not search for an exact set of rules, but consider five helpful steps.
6. The development of a five-year growth program offers the opportunity to do creative planning, to make things happen. Feed your mind with a definite plan and review such plans regularly.
7. Learn to think in terms of your real potential. Re-decide, if

necessary. The actual pursuit of any new adventure is in your hands.

8. Ask yourself, were it not for economic necessity would I be willing to pursue this venture? A happy worker will be a productive worker. Follow six rules for a happy working environment.

9. Do not overlook the little things—when joined together they comprise the big ones.

10. Goals are the spirit of life. Willpower fuels that spirit and absorbs energies. First, build a success consciousness and then build the riches of life.

11. Life is action, the use of one's power. Power is given to you for constructive use. Use it wisely, don't abuse it.

APOTHEGMS

1. *Achievement Quotient rises when actions are supported with worthwhile reasons.*

2. *Achievement Quotient rises with a commitment to greatness.*

3. *Achievement Quotient rises with the habit of striving for excellence.*

4. *Achievement Quotient rises when human potential produces greatest enjoyment.*

5. *Achievement Quotient rises when growth plans are committed to writing.*

6. *Achievement Quotient rises with preparation for new horizons.*

7. *Achievement Quotient rises with the creation of satisfying circumstances.*

8. *Achievement Quotient rises when all the little details are accounted for.*

9. *Achievement Quotient rises with the level of success consciousness.*

10. *Achievement Quotient rises when life's rewards are shared.*

MAY GOD BLESS YOU WITH THE RICHES
OF LOVE, HEALTH, HAPPINESS, PROSPERITY

APPENDIX

Question Review

The questions in each chapter section are assembled for study and review. Each reflects a provoking thought that calls for a meaningful response to raise your achievement quotient. Answer them for yourself, then use them for reference and a method of assessing areas for further study. A "YES" answer indicates strong awareness of needs, high self-esteem, and a desire to excel. A "NO" answer suggests there would be value in rereading the chapter or section for clarity of the intent:

Compassion

CHAPTER 1   HUMANITY POWER

CHECK ANSWER
YES   NO

1. Do you have compassion for people?
2. Do you demonstrate compassion for people?
3. Are you satisfied with your achievement level today?
4. Do you have a positive attitude toward achievement?
5. Is your greatest concern for others?
6. Do you make a serious effort to understand yourself?
7. Do you know what you want out of life?
8. Do you care about many people?
9. Do you consider yourself a model to follow?

253

	YES	NO
10. Do people respond willingly to your guidance?		
11. Do you listen to others' experiences and needs?		
12. Do you willingly offer to help people in need?		

PREPARATION

CHAPTER 2 MIND POWER

13. Could you place a value on your mental bank account?
14. Do you enjoy peace, happiness, the riches of life?
15. Is your self-development on-going?
16. Do you think thoughts of achievement?
17. Are you satisfied with your character image?
18. Are you in tune with your habitual thoughts?

CHAPTER 3 WANT POWER

19. Are your wants clearly defined?
20. Do you attempt to satisfy specific needs?
21. Are you pursuing well defined goals?
22. Are your goals supported by well-thought-out plans?
23. Do you possess stick-to-itiveness?
24. Is your outlook one of happy anticipation?

CHAPTER 4 IMAGERY POWER

25. Do you see images of your goals?
26. Does personal growth match your dreams?
27. Do you control your thinking?
28. Do you pursue life with a positive outlook?
29. Are you aware of the world around you?
30. Are you aware that attire depicts your values?

CHAPTER 5 FITNESS POWER

31. Do you follow a balanced fitness program?
32. Will physical fitness carry you over your goal line?
33. Are you noted for using common sense?
34. Are you building social relationships?
35. Are you drawing on the power of the universe?
36. Are your work and time available balanced?

CHAPTER 6 RESOURCE POWER

37. Do you use all your resources for achievement?
38. Do you practice mind and body conditioning?

	YES	NO
39. Have you got your act together?		
40. Are you an idea person?		
41. Are you developing a cooperative spirit with people?		
42. Do you practice self-restraint?		

CHAPTER 7 COMMUNICATION POWER

	YES	NO
43. Are you an effective speaker?		
44. Are you confident in speaking to groups?		
45. Can you satisfy an audience with words?		
46. Do your messages flow with logic?		
47. Do you present a winning platform style?		
48. Do people laugh at your humor?		
49. Do you supplement your speech with aids?		
50. Are you aware of your weaknesses in speech?		
51. Are your meetings productive?		

Quality

CHAPTER 8 COMPETENCE POWER

	YES	NO
52. Are you fully competent to reach your goals?		
53. Are you preparing to meet tomorrow's challenges?		
54. Do you have the courage to shoulder responsibility?		
55. Are your activities and efforts organized?		
56. Are you a results getter?		
57. Do you give unselfishly of your talents and abilities?		
58. Do you adjust quickly to innovations?		
59. Do you enjoy giving extra effort for others?		
60. Do you possess money consciousness?		
61. Are you preparing for higher plateaus?		
62. Do you treat others as you wish to be treated?		

Delivery

CHAPTER 9

	YES	NO
63. Do you portray a magnetic personality?		
64. Are you developing your personality?		

	YES	NO

65. Do you wear a sunny disposition?
66. Do you generate conversation with ease?
67. Do you help others fulfill their ego needs?
68. Do your friends outnumber your enemies?

CHAPTER 10 ENTHUSIASM POWER

69. Are you excited about raising your AQ?
70. Does attitude toward your goals reflect excitement?
71. Do your actions send out rays of enthusiasm?
72. Do you approach challenges with optimistic thoughts?
73. Do you possess the determination to achieve?
74. Do you reflect the enjoyment of life?

CHAPTER 11 SELF-ESTEEM POWER

75. Do you have a high regard for yourself?
76. Are you mindful of your strengths and weaknesses?
77. Do you carry a picture of self-worth in your mind?
78. Are you continuously expanding your total awareness?
79. Do you generate good feelings about yourself?
80. Are you enjoying a satisfying and fulfilling life?

CHAPTER 12   SELF-CONFIDENCE

81. Are accomplishments a habit with you?
82. Do you believe in your ability?
83. Does your posture reflect courage?
84. Do you set personal standards of excellence?
85. Is your decision batting average satisfactory?
86. Do you reflect confidence in others?

CHAPTER 13 PERSISTENCE POWER

87. Do you persist when the going gets tough?
88. Do you gain momentum before reaching the finish line?
89. Do you improve weaknesses to avoid failure?
90. Do you visualize the consequences of achievement?
91. Are you a patient person?
92. Do setbacks challenge you to take action?

ACHIEVEMENT QUOTIENT

CHAPTER 14   SUCCESS POWER

	YES	NO
93. Do you believe you can raise your achievement level?		
94. Do you support your activities with sound reasons?		
95. Do you make your own opportunities?		
96. Is desire to excel a habit with you?		
97. Are you making the most of your potential?		
98. Are your future plans in written form?		
99. Are you ready to reach out for higher pinnacles?		
100. Are you truly happy in your vocation?		
101. Do you consider all components of new projects?		
102. Do you have the will to succeed?		
103. Do you share achievement rewards with others?